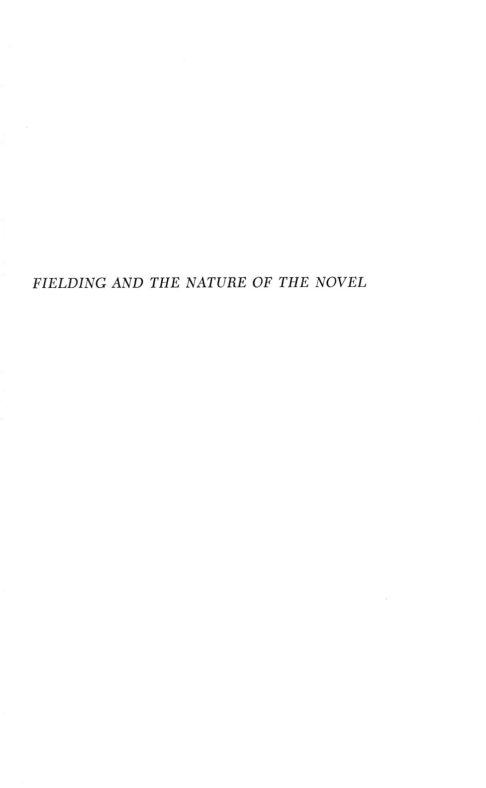

FIELDING AND THE NATURE OF THE NOVEL

FIELDING AND THE

NATURE OF THE NOVEL

Robert Alter

HARVARD UNIVERSITY PRESS

Cambridge, Massachusetts 1968

71265

Very Especially For Judy

PREFACE

The reconsideration of the novels of Henry Fielding attempted here is offered as an essay in the qualification of an accepted critical generalization. Without generalization the act of criticism would be impossible, but generalizations are notoriously treacherous, and none more so than the definition of genres. It is obviously useful to be able to refer individual works to an embracing conception of the genre to which they belong: against a clearly focused background of literary history and generic convention, we can more readily see the creative individuality of the text at hand, how it uses differently what it shares in common with other texts. What happens too often, however, is that critical intelligence is seduced by the shapeliness of the definitions it has inherited or conceived, and as a result it fails to respond adequately to works that cannot be accommodated to the definitions, those very exceptions which, in the proper sense, prove the rule—put it to the test.

Something of this sort, it seems to me, has been the case with critical definitions of the novel and their effects on the estimate of Fielding, and, conversely, with the general failure to use

Fielding, brilliant pioneer of the genre that he is, to enlarge our notion of what the novel may be. It is with this lack in mind that I have turned to Fielding's novels and tried to describe their distinctive achievement, making of them a test case for the adequacy of certain prevalent conceptions of the novel.

The limits of this study are, I trust, distinctly marked off by its title. I do not pretend to offer a comprehensive definition of the whole genre, that great, anomalous literary elephant in the presence of which we are all blind men groping; I have only sought to illuminate those aspects of the genre about which we can learn something from Fielding, the general aspects of the novel that, even apart from any consideration of Fielding, tend to be left in the dark by the supposed beacons of our criticism. Similarly, this is not a comprehensive study of Fielding, his literary sources, the biographical backgrounds of his writing, his relation to the intellectual history of his age, or whatever else might be a legitimate consideration for a full-length scholarly portrait of the man and his work. What I discuss in Fielding is what seems to me important for understanding the nature of his achievement as a novelist, what he reveals through his own artistic practice of the inherent possibilities of the genre.

The idea of the novel as Fielding conceived it must finally be seen in the fulfilled art of just two books—*Joseph Andrews* and *Tom Jones.* Fielding's last novel, *Amelia,* is an only partly realized experiment in a different mode of fiction; what general inferences may be drawn from it are therefore somewhat conjectural. So it seemed appropriate to treat it here separately from the two comic novels, as an unfinished stage in Fielding's lamentably brief career as a novelist. *Jonathan Wild,* on the other hand, has not been included at all in these considerations because it is not really a novel—it belongs instead with *Gulliver's Travels, Candide, Rasselas,* and the other satiric or philosophic fables of the eighteenth century, which are ingenious fictional schematizations of experience in the service of ideas rather than attempts to create through fiction a convincing illusion of life in contemporary society. Over against *Amelia* and *Jonathan Wild*, the two comic novels are mature novelistic achievements that reflect the same underlying conception of the genre. Broadly speaking, one may say that virtually every-thing realized in the art of *Tom Jones* is at least implicit in *Joseph Andrews*, is sometimes merely a simple variation of principles first developed in the earlier novel. For this reason, I have bracketed the two comic novels together and discussed them topically, in terms of function of style, approach to char-acter, and structural unities, always with an eye to what can be inferred from Fielding's handling of these categories about their generic role in the novel.

Since I begin with a polemic against critics who have dis-paraged or dismissed Fielding, something ought to be said here about the admirable work that has been done on Fielding by modern scholarship, especially in the past ten years. If it is still possible to speak of the "neglect" of Fielding in some influential critical circles, almost the opposite is true within the more specialized confines of the academy, where a boom of Fielding scholarship appears to be in full swing. Though I have alluded in the chapters that follow only to the criticism of Fielding which seemed directly relevant to my own purposes, I am of course generally indebted to much of this recent schol-arly activity; occasionally I have built directly upon it, and wherever I was aware of an actual debt or an explicit parallel, I have acknowledged it in text or note. Having said all this, I must add that a great deal has been left undone in develop-ing an intelligent critical terminology for Fielding and the kind of novel he initiated. There have been just two general studies of Fielding as a novelist since the 1920's, both in the last five years, and one is little more than an examination of a series of devices in the novels, while the other reiterates a single self-evident formula instead of articulating an instructive critical argument. With all the scholarly attention, then, that Fielding has received of late, there is still no cogent integral account of his distinctive enterprise as a novelist. It was the hope of offering at least some contribution toward the realization of that goal which led me to undertake this study.

For the sake of simplicity, all quotations are referred to in parenthesis by the book and chapter in which they appear, with occasional indications, where they seemed convenient or necessary, of where in the chapter the given passage occurs. Since the scholarly edition of Fielding's works that is being undertaken by Wesleyan University Press is not yet in print, I have used the texts of the Henley edition (London, 1903), except for *Joseph Andrews*, where Martin Battestin's careful, annotated text (New York, 1961) is available.

This book would not have been possible without the generosity of the John Simon Guggenheim Memorial Foundation and the Columbia University Council for Research in the Humanities. I would also like to thank Professor James Clifford of Columbia University for his kind encouragement, without which I might not have gone on with the whole project. The first chapter was read in draft by Hugh Amory, Edward Said, and Michael Wood, as well as by Professor Clifford, and I am grateful to all of them for their comments and suggestions. As to the rest, I kept close counsel with myself, so that no one else can be held responsible for whatever in these pages may strike a reader as excessive, misguided, or merely wrong. To my wife I am indebted for her patient help in proofreading, and for a much more important kind of patience and support through the entire writing of the book.
Portions of this study first appeared in *Novel* and *Salmagundi*.

New York City
April 1967

CONTENTS

FIELDING AND THE NATURE OF THE NOVEL

*Life isn't long enough to permit
one's giving much time to Fielding.*
—*F. R. Leavis,* The Great Tradition

1. ON THE CRITICAL DISMISSAL OF FIELDING

Fielding, though perennially one of the most popular of the great English novelists, has been treated only sometimes intelligently, and often impatiently, by the critics. Modern critics out of sympathy with Fielding are generally unwilling even to grant him the distinction of monumental failure: they often simply write him off as a popular novelist, in the most limiting, trivializing sense of that term.

As usual, Mr. Leavis offers the sharpest formulation of the attack, innocent of the slightest hint of qualification: "Fielding's attitudes, and his concern with human nature, are simple, and not such as to produce an effect of anything but monotony (on a mind, that is, demanding more than external action) when exhibited at the length of an 'epic in prose.' "[1] The ostensible simplicity of Fielding's concerns with human nature poses a serious problem, one that has bothered many readers. In the present discussion, I shall try to suggest some preliminary answers to this charge, which, however, for full demonstration will have to await a later consideration in detail of Fielding's presentation of character. Mr. Leavis' statement, while it raises a real critical issue, is also colored by a literary prejudice he shares with many modern readers, and it may be worth indicating at the outset precisely what that prejudice is.

Mr. Leavis, like other sophisticated critics of our time, appears to have been brushed by the ghost of old Harry Fielding's hearty Englishness. Fielding, the view implies, may be all right for the casual entertainment of readers who relish foaming English ale, cheery English inns, plump and blushing English wenches, crackling hearthfires, mutton on the spit, and the occasional rousing interlude of a two-fisted free-for-all. But the mature reader will have no patience whatever for all this cosy claptrap, nor for the narrative hocus-pocus of bed-hopping farce and belatedly discovered parentage that goes with it.

Now it is probably true that Fielding has been innocently enjoyed by many readers who were far from subtle, and that even some very good minds have admired him for what may have been the wrong reasons. F. T. Blanchard, the tireless and ultimately tiring chronicler of Fielding's reputation, offers ample evidence to support these assertions in his *Fielding the Novelist*, which traces the writer's critical fortunes until the early 1920's.[2] The evidence is particularly graphic because Blanchard himself is just the sort of admirer of Fielding that modern revisionist critics like Mr. Leavis find so irksome.

Until the beginning of the nineteenth century, Blanchard's study demonstrates, Fielding remained a frequently disparaged second runner to Richardson in critical esteem. He could eclipse his rival only when, with readers like Byron, Hazlitt, and Lamb, England emerged from the morass of rank sentimentality in which—according to Blanchard—it had been wallowing during the latter half of the eighteenth century. This partisan presentation of the facts has the effect of placing special emphasis on something that is in any case largely true for the nineteenth century: that Fielding was mainly admired for his salubriousness. Though the myth of Fielding the rake persisted, not to be completely dispelled until the biographical scholarship of the early twentieth century, readers who preferred him to Richardson sensed something morally bracing in his novels; it made one a better man to read *Tom Jones*—like a vigorous walk before breakfast each day. Similarly, Fielding was praised—often in contrast to Richardson or to the Victorians—for his "realism," a term which seems to mean for the nineteenth century and for Blanchard: English ale, English inns, and so forth. This study of Fielding's reputation, done four decades ago, makes his present neglect in some critical circles quite understandable: the ascendant Fielding of the 1920's portrayed by Blanchard is precisely the old-fashioned Fielding of the 1960's, whose quaint sunlit surfaces must give way once more to the fascinations of Richardson's murky depths, now discovered to anticipate so dramatically the variously excavated depths of the modern psychological novel.

And yet, if one examines the career of Fielding's critical reception more carefully—not to speak of giving the novels themselves closer scrutiny—one begins to suspect that there is something not quite right about this traditional image of the novelist. Although Fielding's fiction has naturally attracted the kind of people who are enthusiastic about hearty old eighteenth-century England, it has also won the ardent admiration of a number of writers in the habit of making far more exacting moral and aesthetic demands upon what they read. Indeed, at some points one almost wonders whether Fielding's popular following and modern detractors, on the one hand, and the more sophisticated of his admirers, on the other hand, have really read the same novelist.

The very writer, for example, whose plots—according to Frank Kermode—"forfeit morality to Sardoodledom," is singled out by as sensitive and probing a moral thinker as Coleridge as a novelist of rare moral insight. The Fielding casually discarded by Leavis because of the appalling simplicity of his attitudes has been snatched up by no less a connoisseur of complexity than William Empson, who extols Fielding for the artful ambiguity of his irony.[3]

This peculiar disparity in critical opinion on the moral worth of Fielding's fiction is reflected as well in the judgments upon his technical accomplishments. Thus Ian Watt, in his otherwise illuminating book on the beginnings of the English novel, can find no significant—or genuinely novelistic—innovation of technique in Fielding's work; so that his desire to be fair-minded ultimately reduces him to praising Fielding in oddly nineteenth-century terms for his "wisdom."[4] Yet André Gide, among modern novelists a writer so extraordinarily preoccupied with technique, could be struck with envying admiration for the technical achievement of *Tom Jones* while working on his own most ambitious experiment in novelistic technique. In his entry for February 14, 1924, in the *Journal des Faux-Monnayeurs,* Gide writes: "I again find myself confronted with my *Counterfeiters,* but this brief plunge into Fielding enlightens me on the inadequacies of my book. I wonder whether I shouldn't enlarge the text, intervene . . . comment." [5]

It would of course be fatuous to undertake a rehabilitation of Fielding by citing critical authorities. My intention in listing "testimonials" is merely to suggest that there may be certain odd and perhaps instructive discrepancies in the reading habits of highly literate people if Fielding can mean so much to some acute readers while he is of such little consequence to many serious modern critics that he scarcely deserves to be attacked, only dismissed or ignored. Fielding, who was to a large extent a victim of the critical orthodoxies of his contemporaries—and consequently, then as now, a popular novelist but not altogether a respected one—has, it seems to me, suffered from modern critical orthodoxies of a subtler, less avowed kind. He is virtually left out of the realm of the English novel by some critics largely because his writing does not correspond to a number of tacitly shared, more or less unquestioned assumptions about the nature and purpose of fiction and the fictional treatment of moral experience. These assumptions, moreover, bear a surprisingly direct relationship to the tenets of the fashionable eighteenth-century critics who greeted Fielding's novels on their appearance with lofty disdain.

The most articulate and forceful spokesman for the opposition to Fielding among his contemporaries is, of course, Samuel Johnson. It may be worthwhile to review briefly Johnson's objections to Fielding and to consider what underlying attitudes they imply in order to determine whether any of the objections or the attitudes behind them persist in informed literary opinion today. Johnson wrote nothing on Fielding; but in his recorded conversation three specific reasons for his disapproval of Fielding recur: Fielding's characters are, in a strictly descriptive sense of the word, superficial; Fielding's fiction, with the exception of *Amelia,* is morally reprehensible; Fielding's subjects are unconscionably "low."

The last of these objections is the one that can most easily be set aside as the expression of an eighteenth-century prejudice to which no one subscribes any more. Neoclassical aesthetic principle leads Johnson to think that serious literature should be dignified—certain kinds of reality and language ought to be excluded. By now, of course, the nethermost varieties of realistic lowness are so fully respectable in the novel that no modern critic could conceivably object to Fielding on this ground. The other two reasons for Johnson's opposition to Fielding are moral, or moral-aesthetic, rather than social-aesthetic, and here Johnson shows a virtual identity of attitudes with Fielding's great rival, Richardson. That is, Johnson the common-sense moralist and Christian humanist in these objections to Fielding thinks and feels in the terms of what is now usually called "the Puritan imagination." And the same largely holds true, as we shall see, for the modern critics of the novel who have relegated Fielding to the limbo of quaintly ornamental literary bric-a-brac.

The vehemence of Johnson's moral opposition to Fielding is not at first easy to account for. When Hannah More mentioned *Tom Jones* to him, he rebuked her for reading "so vicious a book," and told her, in a statement sweeping even for him, "I scarcely know a more corrupt work." [6] What could have seemed so disturbingly corrupt to Johnson in a book that, with its dastardly villains, golden-hearted benefactors, and final Just Deserts for all, has struck many modern readers as a piece of old-fashioned moralizing? I suspect that the lurking moral horror for Johnson in Fielding's sunny landscape was Tom's sexual adventures. Johnson was certainly no prude, but sex was ultimately a serious matter for him. With his sense of the darknesses below in human nature, the restraining or limiting of sexual impulse was an imposing challenge, perhaps at times a threatening one. If such restraint broke down, so might "subordination" itself—the whole precarious dike that Christian ethics had shored up against man's potential for chaos.

At first glance, such a view on Johnson's part might seem to separate him from modern critics—who come after the so-called sexual revolution—even more decisively than his objections to lowness in the novel. But the particular moral judgment one places on an activity like fornication may not be so significant as the amount of emotional energy one directs toward the idea. The aspect of *Tom Jones* that I think most bothers Johnson and perhaps some readers today is that while sexual activity in the course of the novel is frequent, usually pleasant, and often amusing, it is not ultimately important, nor fraught with irrevocable and far-reaching moral consequences. Johnson's sense of corruptness in *Tom Jones* stems not only from the fact that Fielding fails to punish Tom for his imprudent sexual escapades, but also from Fielding's general representation of sex, promiscuous or otherwise, as skylarking, not skirting the abyss.

As Richardson's greatest novel illustrates so memorably, sex mattered for the Puritan imagination. Though direct reference to it was ordinarily to be avoided, it loomed tremendous in the backgound, the law of the return of the repressed working with a vengeance. It is not an exaggeration to say that in *Clarissa* sex progressively engulfs life, until it becomes equivalent to all of life and death as well for the two central characters. Though Fielding was deeply impressed by *Clarissa*, his own sharply contrasting sense of the place of sex in the general scheme of things is made clear by a barbed comment on *Pamela* which he places in the first mock introductory letter to his parody *Shamela:* "The comprehensiveness of his imagination must be truly prodigious! It has stretched out this mere grain of mustard-seed (a poor girl's little, &c.) into a resemblance of that Heaven, which the best of good books has compared it to."

What Fielding caught Richardson doing unawares with the sexuality of his characters in *Pamela* is precisely what many serious modern novelists have set out to do quite consciously in their fiction. Sex, in the healthier of our novelists, is no longer threatening or Satanic, but the Puritan feeling persists that sex is something portentous, involving man's ultimate moral responsibilities, leading him if not to damnation then perhaps to his greatest fulfillment, to "that Heaven, which the best of good books has compared it to." To a critic for whom D. H. Lawrence, for example, is one of the great English novelists, it is understandable that Fielding's treatment of sex should seem—not disturbing, as for Johnson—but trivial and superficial. A novelist who imagines those great, dark passional aspects of the psyche as nothing more than the impetus for a romp in the haystack obviously does not take life very seriously. What is usually obscured but ought to be made clear is that such criticism is being conducted upon a definite moral bias: if the Puritan imagination has had an immeasurable impact on the English novel, its influence on the criticism of the English novel is probably at least as pervasive though perhaps not always so obvious.

This influence is probably at the bottom of the objection to Fielding most unequivocally shared by Johnson and the moderns: the complaint about the externality of Fielding's characterization or the simplicity of his grasp of human nature. One can, of course, enjoy Fielding's gay ironies on sex and yet find grave fault with his presentation of character. But, from Johnson's time to ours, the objections to Fielding's treatment of sex and to his understanding of human nature have been typically associated in a single complex of values. This is not to suggest that Puritan moral seriousness derives from a preoccupation with sex, only that the one attitude generally implies the other. Johnson's formulation of his own sense of the superficiality in Fielding is brief and emphatic: "There is all the difference in the world between characters of nature and characters of manners; and *there* is the difference between the characters of Fielding and those of Richardson. Characters of manners are very entertaining; but they are to be understood, by a more superficial observer, than characters of nature, where a man must dive into the recesses of the human heart." [7]

Though Johnson's critical terminology may be strange to us, his conception of literature and reality is strikingly modern. "Characters of manners" are characters patterned upon social stereotypes: the novelist looks sharply around him in society, and with what meets the eye and strikes the ear, he composes his squires, parsons, hostlers, innkeepers—vividly fresh yet familiar figures. "Nature" in Johnson's statement, as so often in eighteenth-century writers, means something like "accurately perceived human nature." One might modernize "characters of nature" to "characters of psychological depth and complexity." Johnson's own use of the familiar metaphor of depth is revealing. On several occasions he asserted that, in comparison to Richardson, Fielding knew nothing of the heart, but here we get some intimation of how one goes about acquiring a knowledge of the heart: a man must dive into deep recesses. There is, in Johnson's view, something perhaps ominously opaque at the core of human nature which plain reason cannot be expected to penetrate. In effect Johnson is describing not merely two different kinds of characters but two very different creative processes for writing novels. On the one hand, reportorial observation and the analytic and synthetic exercise of the intellect produce a *Tom Jones*. On the other hand, a process is at work which we might call, in our own jargon, creative insight or creative intuition. The writer feels his way imaginatively into the dark corners of the self and projects characters out from it: fed by the novelist's own resinous heart, a Lovelace, an Ahab, a Raskolnikov, a Kurtz, flames out on the night of human understanding.

It begins to be apparent why many modern readers concur with Johnson in insisting that Richardson's visceral relationship to his characters produces greater fiction than Fielding's more cerebral connection with the figures he invents. But it may be instructive to examine in detail a central modern statement of critical depreciation of Fielding to see exactly what has happened to Johnson's ideas in the passage of two centuries. Most recent critics antipathetic to Fielding have apparently observed Mr. Leavis' admonition about the brevity of life, but some years ago Frank Kermode fortunately took the time to devote a thoughtful essay in the *Cambridge Journal* to that perennial subject, "Richardson and Fielding." [8]

Kermode sees Fielding's characterization substantially as Johnson did, though the terms he uses reflect a greater concern with the formal categories of history of literature. What Johnson calls characters of manners are for Kermode the result of "the neo-classical habit of stylization learned in the theatre." That is, the novelist, instead of creating from within highly individualized imaginative entities, simply draws upon the ready resource of "genre- and type-characterization." This is more or less justified for Fielding's minor characters but is certainly overstated for most of the major ones. Surely there is a real difference in kind between the wooden conventionality of the booby squire familiar to Fielding from post-Restoration comedy and the explosive vitality of a Squire Western.

But if Kermode's description of Fielding's characters is—like Johnson's—a little too confidently neat, his notion of Richardson's characters is suggestive. He reformulates the idea of characters of nature in a way that illuminates an important modern attitude toward fiction and incidentally supplies an intriguing commentary on the meaning of that "knowledge of the heart" which Johnson praised in Richardson's novels. For Kermode, Richardson towers over Fielding because of his "mythopoeic procedure" of novel writing, a procedure which in characterization produces an "archetypal integration of character and motive."

The desirability of integrating character and motive is self-evident, and we shall have to return to the question of Fielding's imputed failure to effect this integration. What is particularly interesting in Kermode's formulation is the emphasis he places on myth and archetype in describing what he thinks of as the highest kind of achievement in fiction. "Mythopoeic" is certainly an apt word to use for Richardson's method, as Dorothy Van Ghent's analysis of *Clarissa* has since so brilliantly illustrated.[9] But one may question the implication that literature of an authentically mythic nature is somehow superior to literature devoid of serious myth.

It is hardly a secret that we live in a myth-conscious age. Our literary world bears witness to this fact in the enthusiastic following enjoyed by critics like Leslie Fiedler and Northrop Frye, by novelists like Conrad, Kafka, and, recently, William

Golding. I think it is a modest and reasonable contention that myth provides a legitimate way, but by no means the only legitimate way, of looking at a man or representing him in literature. It sets a man against the background of his whole race, measures his movements by the rhythms of the cosmic processes. The mythopoeic imagination sees the individual not so much as a man among other men at a particular time and place, but as a recapitulation of mankind's past and perhaps also a rehearsal of its future. In a curious way the modern devotees of mythic analysis have followed the guideposts of Jung and Freud to a position on the eternal oneness of human nature that is surprisingly like Johnson's distinctly eighteenth-century view. Johnson's praise of the "just representations of general nature" in Shakespeare might almost be used to introduce a modern analysis of archetypal patterns in Shakespeare's plays: "His characters are not modified by the customs of particular places . . . or by the accidents of transient fashions or temporary opinions: . . . [they] act and speak by the influence of those general passions and principles by which all minds are agitated, and the whole system of life is continued in motion." [10] It is clear that such a view, whether grounded in neoclassical aesthetics or archetypal psychology, is not likely to generate sympathy for the novel that deals in the varying textures and contours of social life.

But just as important in the vogue of myth as this quest for oneness amidst the variety of life and art is the conviction that the ultimate truths about human nature are arrived at not by intellection but by diving into recesses where the real springs of thought and action lie hidden in prerational, subconscious gloom. A loss of faith in the daylight rational world is perfectly understandable, especially in a century whose history has proved to be such a long nightmare with no waking up in prospect. But it ought to be recognized as a belief about human life and not imagined as an absolute

criterion by which all literature can be judged. It is hard to
see, for example, why Pope's *Fourth Dunciad* should be a
greater poem than his *Second Moral Essay* simply because,
in contrast to the *Moral Essay,* its imagination is mythopoeic,
or because it has none of the confidence of the earlier poem
that reason will prevail against the destructive threat of
human irrationality.

Our general assumptions about man, reason, and society
have obviously shifted in a radical way since Fielding's time
—and, for that matter, he himself was perhaps a little old-
fashioned in his own age. Kermode, like other modern critics,
is altogether impatient with Fielding's moral criterion of the
Good Heart, and no doubt all of us must have other thoughts
about the human heart after Dachau and Auschwitz. Few
readers now will find Fielding as morally relevant as novelists
with a more brooding sense of man's potential for evil, but
to say that a writer's world view differs from the prevalent
modern one surely does not have to mean that he is superficial.
It is just this distinction, though, which some modern critics
fail to make. Arnold Kettle, at the beginning of an otherwise
misguided reading of *Tom Jones,* describes nicely the intervention of moral antipathy in critical judgment. Fielding, he
says, "is not complacent but he is fundamentally confident
that the problems of human society, that is to say, *his* society,
can and will be solved by humane feeling and right reason.
It is this broad and tolerant confidence which gives *Tom
Jones* its particular tone and which also (one suspects) alienates
those critics who feel less confidence in social man than Fielding, whose optimism they mistake for insensitiveness." [11]

When a critic of the kind Kettle has in mind happens to
be morally out of phase with the work he is discussing, he
runs the danger of underreading, so that he may miss much
of the intellectual and artistic activity that actually goes on
in the text. Then, by studying his own two-dimensional mental

snapshots of a three-dimensional literary work, he ends by transferring his original lack of moral sympathy into ostensibly formal, or technical, criticism. (The performances of some of the more vehement anti-Miltonists offer one clear illustration of how the process works.) In this connection, Kermode's essay is a particularly interesting document because his critique of Fielding's novelistic procedures, while giving the appearance of great care and even subtlety, is guilty, I think, of certain serious errors in reading and judgment.

A novel, Kermode assumes, involves the revelation of moral character through action. Fielding's unforgivable fault is the dissociation of character from conduct: he first decides who among his characters are unspeakable villains, who men of Good Heart; then he proceeds to manipulate them in a plot entirely external to them, with no action they can perform being allowed to modify the a priori judgment of their moral worth. The result is a superficial, evasive approach to moral questions in the novel and a meretricious narrative "technique" that is little more than a series of juggler's stunts. To support this reading of Fielding, Kermode cites two familiar episodes from *Tom Jones:* Tom's misapprehension of having committed incest in his encounter with Mrs. Waters (XVIII, 2) and Blifil's setting free the beloved pet bird of Sophia (IV, 3). He sees the former incident, where the goodness of a good character is involved, as an instance of Fielding's failure to imagine the moral implications of his hero's actions or of his own plot, while the bird-freeing episode, where the badness of a bad character is in question, is taken as an example of the complete insulation of the writer's moral judgment on his characters from the character's actions. Both interpretations illustrate how the characteristically modern lack of sympathy with Fielding's aims impedes intelligent reading. In one case, it leads to an insistence that the novelist conform to a rigid preconceived standard of what novel writing should be; in the other case, it causes even so perceptive a critic as Kermode to mistake seriously much of what Fielding plainly says.

Let us consider first the scare Tom has over Mrs. Waters. Precisely what is it in this farcical brush with the fate of Oedipus that reveals the hopeless moral superficiality of the novel to Kermode? "Now the flesh and spirit of Jones," he begins, "are matters of common observation; but his good luck is not." We may pause to wonder whether the observation in question is so common as to be false. In the most offhand, conversational way, one might point a Pauline finger at the willingness of Tom's spirit, the weakness of his flesh. But what Fielding actually shows us in the novel is a hero whose "spirit" is just what leads him into the bushes with Molly Seagrim, into a midnight assignation with Mrs. Waters, and even—alas—into being kept by Lady Bellaston. The interesting moral point made through the character of Tom is the denial of spirit–flesh dichotomies: Tom's exuberant sexuality is closely associated with his impulsive generosity (that is, the Good Heart), his sometimes misguided sense of honor, his general vitality, moral as well as physical. The imprudent but thoroughly male sensibility which leads him to accept Lady Bellaston's dubious "challenge" is merely a misdirected expression of the very qualities that make him a perfect husband for Sophia. But Kermode assumes that Fielding must be simple, so he bases his critique of the mock-incest episode on a simplistic popular conception of Fielding's moral views. He has, however, an interesting point of his own to make in objecting to the way the imagined catastrophe is averted: "Fielding the moralist completely evades the only genuine crucial test that confronts his character as a moral being in the whole course of his adventures. The Comic Spirit has intervened, as usual theatrically, to solve what is essentially a theatrically simple dualism of character."

The only reasonable construction I can put on these words

is that the writer feels Mrs. Waters really should have been Tom's mother, so that his sexual adventurism would in fact lead him eventually into the unsupportable horror of incest. The usually diffuse influence of Puritanism on the English critical imagination here gathers to an almost painful concentration. Kermode would of course not say that sexual promiscuity must be punished by a novelist, only that its serious moral consequences should be made apparent—by bringing this amorous young scamp to bed with his mother! (We are perilously close here to the hair-raising comment on Lot's incestuous daughters by a third-century rabbi: "Whoever is too hungry for sexual pleasure will end up being fed from his own flesh.") Putting aside the brimstone morality to which this kind of critical stricture might lead, we ought to consider for a moment what has been assumed about the nature of fictional experience.

The key phrase, I think, is "genuine crucial test." The critic presupposes that life as it is represented in fiction should above all be morally problematic. The protagonist of any novel that is more than superficial ought to be confronted with a series of moral tests. Life, in this fashionable modern critical vision of it, is an unrelenting trial in which the individual's moral salvation or damnation is hanging continually and precariously in the balance. Man appears very much as he was imagined by the Puritans and translated into fiction by Richardson: a battleground where God and Satan struggle tensely for domination.

One immediate result of this particular conception of fiction is that it precludes the possibility of a comic novel. And Kermode's condescending reference to the Comic Spirit is a further indication that he denies the basic legitimacy of what Fielding has set out to achieve both in this particular episode and in his novel as a whole. For the main point in adding the threat of incest to Tom Jones's abundant though temporary miseries is precisely to underscore the generic difference between tragedy and the kind of fiction this novel is meant to be. Fielding brings his story here as close as possible to the archetypal tragic situation in order to remind us that his comic novel may parody tragedy but can never actually get involved in it.

The tongue-in-cheek chapter heading, "Containing a Very Tragical Incident," signals at once the ironic perspective in which we are supposed to see the ostensibly horrifying events of the chapter. Tom's reaction to the soul-shattering revelation by Partridge is not, as some modern readers may conclude, an instance of the inept rendering of emotional experience through exclamatory rhetoric. On the contrary, it is an artfully contrived parody of the tragic hero's response to his tragic discovery. "Oh, good Heavens! incest," Tom cries, and then deflates the pretended solemnity of the moment by his comically obtuse addition, "—with a mother!" When he follows these words with the standard miserable hero's formula, "To what am I reserved?" and a good bout of violent throes and thrashings-about, we should be careful not to rush to the conclusion of Ian Watt and others that Fielding has simply waded out of his depth. There is certainly evidence enough in the passage to suggest that the absurdity of the verbal and physical gesticulations has been planned by the novelist for comic effect.

What we are made aware of, then, as the shadow of incest passes over Tom, is that in his world it could only be a threatening shadow without substance. By bringing his narrative to the imagined brink of tragedy, Fielding calls special attention to his strategy in the novel as a whole: to transmit all action through the medium of a knowing, beneficent narrator whose presence creates for the reader, as Wayne Booth has put it, "a kind of comic analogue of the true believer's reliance on a benign providence in real life." [12] Fielding in this way has worked out a technical device for building into his narrative the providential quality that inheres in most comic worlds and which he, more conscious of the distinctions between literary kinds than we generally are today, would have kept very much in mind. It may be objected that life is not like this, but what that really means is that life is no comedy. Perhaps that is so: Richardson, Richardson's Puritan predecessors, and the Richardsonian critics would certainly concur. But if comedy is ultimately wish-fulfillment, at its greatest it is clearly wish-fulfillment of a liberating, morally illuminating sort. In Fielding, moreover, some of the illumination comes from the author's continuous awareness that comedy itself is an artifact, a container for experience that might also be tragic. The incest episode touches upon this idea playfully; later, in the prefatory chapter to Book XVII, the narrator states more explicitly that it is a decision of art which turns ambiguous life into either tragedy or comedy.

In any case, the necessarily privileged status enjoyed by the comic hero as a kind of natural child of the gods does not lend itself to the revelation of the moral meanings of the comedy through crucially "testing" situations. With the partial exception of *Amelia,* this is obviously not the way Fielding intended to write his novels. He had other means— often overlooked by his critics—for bringing complex moral perspectives to bear on the people and events of his narrative.

An example of some of the procedures Fielding uses to thicken his moral plot is the very incident of Sophia's pet bird which Kermode uses to illustrate the novelist's shallow conception of character and morality. The episode, a kind of final preface to the main action of the novel, takes place when Tom, Blifil, and Sophia are in their early teens. The songbird named Tommy, a present from the young Jones to Sophia, has become her chief occupation and delight. While the Allworthy family with its pedagogues is paying a visit to the Westerns, Blifil seizes an opportune moment to free the bird. Sophia screams with dismay; Tom scrambles up a tree in pursuit of the bird and, when the bough breaks, is doused in a canal; then Blifil explains his action by pleading compassion for the cruelly confined bird which had languished for its liberty.

There is no question that Fielding thinks Tom an admirable, compassionate, courageous young man in this incident, while Blifil is an unmanly scoundrel. And it is just this judgment which Kermode sees as proof of the split between character and conduct in *Tom Jones*: Blifil must be villainous in Fielding's eyes despite the fact that he is performing a humanitarian act. The novel, of course, makes it quite clear that there is nothing humanitarian in what Blifil does. This precisely illustrates the peculiar fate Fielding sometimes suffers in our age: he is hardly a writer who requires esoteric disciplines in order to be understood, yet some modern critical biases lead to willful misreading by intelligent readers.

Now, this whole distinction between character and conduct originates in an observation on Fielding made by Coleridge, but Kermode has curiously simplified Coleridge's nice differentiation and thus deflected praise of Fielding into a wrongheaded objection to his method. Here is Coleridge's own comment on the liberation of Sophia's bird: "If I want a servant or mechanic, I wish to know what he does:—but of a friend, I must know what he is. And in no writer is this momentous distinction so finely brought forward as by Fielding. We do not care what Blifil does;—the deed, as separate from the agent, may be good or ill; but Blifil is a villain; and we feel him to be so from the very moment he, the boy Blifil, restores Sophia's poor captive bird to its native and rightful liberty." [13]

Coleridge is obviously not suggesting that what a person does is generally unrelated to what he is. But the relationship, he reminds us, is never absolute. This caution is vitally important in connection with those we care for, both because it would be morally unthinkable to regard them as instruments and because, given the general state of human imperfection, love would hardly survive if it were strictly dependent upon performance. In the light of Coleridge's analysis, Sophia's persisting love for Tom may seem less like an improbable narrative convention, more like a humanly understandable response to an upright man and his mixed-up actions.

Of equal importance in Coleridge's observation is the implication that Fielding, by distinguishing between deed and doer, focuses our attention on the often perplexed problem of the motives for particular actions and the moral contexts in which they occur. What this means in terms of narrative technique is that Fielding shifts the onus of crucial decision from the characters to the reader, who is called upon to play the role of judge while the novelist presents evidence, both relevant and misleading, and opinions, right, wrong, or otherwise, about the characters and their deeds.[14] Fielding differs from later novelists—George Eliot, say, or Henry James—in that he approaches these questions of motive and moral judgment by giving the reader data to infer from, not by analyzing the characters himself or by presenting their own introspective self-analysis. The moral complexity of the novel, then, consists not in choices to be made by the protagonists but in the qualifying contexts of actions and in the range of attitudes we are invited to take toward the actions. The dichotomy in Fielding's fiction is not an inadvertent one of conduct and character but an artfully contrived dichotomy between actions—which are relatively simple—and the possible constructions that can be put on the actions.

The case of the freed bird, in comparison to others in *Tom Jones,* is fairly simple to judge. We immediately suspect that Blifil's motives are far from humanitarian if we note that he asks for Sophia's pet only upon "observing the extreme fondness that she showed for the bird." His actual intention is in fact perfectly realized when the bird is carried off by a hawk as Jones tumbles into the canal.

The chapter immediately following extends the process of

judicial deliberation in which Fielding means to involve his reader—and this is one good reason for the chapter heading: "Containing Such Very Deep and Grave Matters, that Some Readers, Perhaps, May Not Relish It." The Deep and Grave Matters are in effect a formal debate on the rightness of Blifil's action. Thwackum and Square argue the religious or ethical grounds for the liberation of the bird; Allworthy logically (and naively) infers Blifil's generous motives from the facts of the case; Squire Western's unreflective impulsiveness, which so often leads him to wild misconceptions, here keeps him from being put off by the hypocritical show, and it is he who pronounces the soundest judgment on Blifil. The debate on the moral status of the action is concluded with an opinion from a handily present lawyer on whether Blifil's freeing the bird is legally theft. Legal opinion, like the consensus of the debate, appears to favor Blifil, but is not entirely conclusive.

It is tempting but unwise to grow too ardent in waving the modern banner of complexity over Fielding's novels. In the episode we are considering, it is clear that the "complexity" is limited to involving the reader in an intellectual activity of judgment, while the verdict he is asked to issue is plain and unambiguous. Such untroubled certainty is by no means the response Fielding intends to elicit in all the moral questions raised by his novels, but it is the characteristic attitude he takes toward his villains—who are rather a special case in his moral world. In any event, the black judgment we are invited to pass on Blifil the Bird Lover is more than a self-righteous exercise of damning a damnable scoundrel. The whole episode of the escaped bird is, of course, a symbolic introduction to the main events of the novel. As such, it is meant to guide our reading of the novel—and in one respect, to misguide as well—by presenting schematically the relationship between Tom and Sophia, between Blifil and each of the lovers, and also by giving us a sort of diagrammatic illustration of Blifil's hypocrisy at work.

The boy Blifil drives the bird named Tommy from its happy captivity in the hands of Sophia, just as the young man Blifil will bring about the expulsion of Tom from the Allworthy estate and hence from his beloved. Blifil is moved to slip the string from the bird's leg out of envious spite for Jones and a delight in inflicting pain upon Sophia. (Later, in VII, 6, Fielding will suggest in chilling terms the plainly sadistic aspect of Blifil's desire for Sophia: "this [her aversion for him] served rather to heighten the pleasure he proposed in rifling her charms, as it added triumph to lust; nay, he had some further views, from the absolute possession of her person, which we detest too much even to mention; and revenge itself was not without its share in the gratifications which he promised himself.") While Blifil the liberator of captive birds acts just as Blifil the unwelcome suitor will act later, the bird itself is very much like its namesake in its mercurial imprudence: "The foolish animal no sooner perceived itself at liberty than, forgetting all the favours it had received from Sophia, it flew directly from her."

After marking out the path of the novel in this careful fashion, Fielding makes certain to drag a couple of red herrings across the track. Little Tommy's precarious freedom ends under the talons of a hawk, while the law seems to be on Blifil's side; later, of course, the human Tom's adventures will for a time threaten to end on a scaffold through a collusion between the law and Blifil's villainy. And the death of the bird, as a careful parody of the Homeric use of bird omens, strikes precisely the light note of supposedly impending fate which Fielding needs to introduce the main action of his comic epic. Once acquainted with the incident of Sophia's bird and the debate that follows it, we are properly prepared to read the novel. And immediately after the last words of the debate, the narrative leaps ahead in time to the beginning of the principal action (IV, 5): the novel's exposition has been concluded with these two chapters that symbolically prefigure the rest of the book, and now the main plot is ready to unwind.

There is, I think, an important point to be learned from all this about how one should read Fielding. Because the author of *Tom Jones* is so obviously and often spectacularly a stylist, he has been accused—again, most pointedly by Kermode—of being complex merely in texture while deficient in structure. That is, the much vaunted plot of *Tom Jones* is well-made, but only as a *pièce bien faite*, a contrived entertainment. What this accusation fails to allow for is the fact that Fielding's elaborate craftsmanship is not limited to keeping a clockwork plot mechanism ticking. Fielding's structures, like his textures, yield meaning. The symmetries and balanced antitheses of the plot of *Tom Jones*, the ingenious doublings and reversals of roles and situations and symbols, provide the reader with a set of multiple, mutually qualifying perspectives in which to view the moral action of the novel. In the chapters that follow, these systems of interrelationship will be examined in detail.

All three of Fielding's novels, but most clearly *Tom Jones*, were written to be read ideally in the way we have been reading the so-called art novel since the time of Conrad and James. Each book is an intricate reflexive system that cannot be fully grasped with only one reading. Even in the relatively simple instance of Sophia's bird, not only does the episode affect our reading of all that follows, but our retrospective awareness of what follows influences our understanding of what actually happened in the early episode. No incident or action can be discussed in isolation from its context in the novel as a whole without at least partly distorting its meaning.

It is not really surprising that modern critics accustomed to reading novels in just this fashion should so often misread

Fielding. Slapdash comic playwright, Grub Street journalist, genial old eighteenth-century essayist and humanist, by tradition he is hopelessly entangled with all those qualities that in our popular mental image typify the literature of his age and divide it from ours. The entanglement goes back in one respect to Fielding's own contemporaries, some of whom imagined *Tom Jones* and *Roderick Random* to be the work of the same writer. Such a mistake could only have been made by failing to see the overwhelming difference between Smollett's practice of writing novels as freehand narrative improvisations and Fielding's conception of the novel as a work of art. The notion of Fielding as a kind of Smollett with fancier style and more fastidious nose has vaguely persisted. For some of the reasons I have tried to trace above, many critics of our age have had little inclination to test the validity of this tradition by giving Fielding a really fresh reading.

It would be foolish to argue for the intrinsic superiority of Fielding's kind of novel to others. Fielding is different from Richardson, not necessarily better or worse. With all his artistic sophistication, there are clearly realms of experience that his kind of writing and his kind of sensibility cannot reach. But what should be avoided by intelligent criticism is to canonize one particular variety of the novel. Even so excellent a book as Ian Watt's *The Rise of the Novel* tends to have that effect, and the canonization of one kind is just a step from the policy of Mr. Leavis, which is to excommunicate all others. It is certainly curious that of the influential English writers whom we periodically relegate to antiquity, one often chosen is that eighteenth-century novelist who made the greatest conscious use of the resources of style and structure, who conceived novel reading as a vigorous intellectual activity, and who imagined the genre he was helping to shape as a serious form of art. How he put his resources to use, how he realized his high conception of the genre, will be the subject of the rest of this study.

Writing well is at the same time perceiving well, thinking well, and saying well.
—*Buffon*

2. THE USES OF STYLE

There is a kind of paradox inherent in the way language characteristically works in the novel. In some respects, words become more important than they ever were in the traditional genres. This importance, qualitative as well as quantitative, is partly a function of the uniquely commercial basis of the novel as a genre: many novelists, after all, have been paid for the number of words they produced, whether wholesale, for a printer, or in retail installments, for serial publication. Writers of novels, moreover, who have not depended on the favor of a patron or coterie but largely on the precarious good will and dubious comprehension of the newly literate middle classes, often have felt constrained to take scrupulous care that all the words they used should be both broadly understandable and unlikely to give offense. In any case, the novel, youngest of the major genres and the only one whose whole history follows the advent of printing, is intended, as all good children once were, mainly to be seen and not heard, and this means that in it, by contrast to the older genres whose origins are oral, the word is always exposed in the shining nakedness of its printed form, where the solitary reader can ponder at leisure its force, its implications, its decorousness, and is even at liberty to scrutinize the grossness or niceties of its typographical shape. Yet, with all this heightened consciousness of the verbal medium, language has been typically used by one dominant tradition of the novel in ways meant to foster the illusion of its own absence.

It has been suggested that the function of language in the novel is more strictly representational than it is in other genres. On reflection, this distinction seems less than precise. Is the language Homer uses to describe the infant Astyanax shrinking in fright from his helmeted father Hector, or that with which the biblical narrator reports Joseph's relevation to his brothers in Egypt, really less representational than, say, Balzac's language in his account of the Goriot daughters emoting over their father's deathbed, or Arnold Bennett's when he depicts the reunion, after twenty years' separation, between Sophia and Constance Baines? Novelists, of course, do tend to develop their representation of such human events through the specification of minute, even trivial particulars of everyday experience, but this distinguishes what they write from the older narrative genres primarily in terms of the kinds or quantities of materials selected from reality, not in terms of the relationship of language to reality.

It would be more accurate to say that language in the novel often tries to disguise its own status as artifice, aspiring to an ideal and impossible condition of complete transparency in which our attention would be wholly fixed on the objects represented and entirely averted from the verbal medium through which the representation takes place. This is the implicit logic of the development of the novel from beginnings in pseudo-documentary forms—confessions, letters, journals, memoirs—to the sophisticated representation of consciousness, whether the narration immerses us in its stream or watches perched high and dry on a Jamesian post of observation.

Novelists, as we so often say, like to have us "enter into" their characters, and from Moll Flanders' autobiography to Molly Bloom's oceanic night thoughts, from Clarissa Harlowe's letters to Clarissa Dalloway's interior monologues, writers of novels have invented strategies to help us pretend that the inevitable partition of literary artifice separating reader from character was not really there. Even when a novelist's language is obtrusively stylized, the stylization itself frequently proves to be an attempt at reproducing the immediacy of inner experience, as the elaborate hesitation dance of the later James's prose adumbrates the superfine labyrinthine consciousness of his protagonists or as the excited lyric pulsations of Virginia Woolf's prose are an attempt to approximate what she conceives to be the essentially lyric nature of consciousness itself.

The aspiration, moreover, to a transparent medium is not entirely limited to novelists preoccupied with getting inside their characters' minds. In many novels, what happens to and between personages is reported so directly and efficiently that we are invited by the discreet mode of presentation to attend solely to what is happening, not to who is narrating or how. This is surely the general effect of Smollett's brisk, detached, facilely elegant style, almost everywhere the same in tone and manner; it is what leads Balzac to give page after page of uninterrupted dialogue, without so much as a "he said" or "she said" to remind us of the author's presence; and it is what Trollope has in mind when in his *Autobiography* he denounces the contortions of Dickens' prose and the convolutions of George Eliot's while insisting on the importance of plain and clear language in the novel.

Language, however, stubbornly refuses to efface itself, and so, from the earliest stage of the genre, there have been novelists who have taken care to call our attention, boldly, playfully, ingeniously, melodramatically, sometimes just uneasily, to the words out of which their fictional worlds were created.

Joyce's *Ulysses,* in this respect as in others, is a recapitulation of the history of the genre because it represents a culmination of *both* traditions—using language as a transparent medium and using language as a figured glass through which light shows in elaborate formal patterns. No narrator has been so extraordinarily invisible and so raucously, self-consciously conspicuous as the narrator of *Ulysses,* who flaunts or hides his presence from section to section and sometimes actually manages to do both at once. If the erotic fantasies of Richardson's Lovelace begin the novelistic mode that eventuates in Bloom's mental voyages to the seraglio, Joyce's virtuoso handling of the novel as formal poetic vehicle, verbal vaudeville, parody, self-parody, mock-epic, serious comic epic, variation on classical myth, looks back for its first and greatest English predecessor in all these respects to the novels of Henry Fielding.

When Fielding, in both the Preface to *Joseph Andrews* and in the prefatory chapters of *Tom Jones,* speaks of the genre he is inventing ("this kind of writing, which I do not remember to have seen hitherto attempted in our language") as a comic variant of the Homeric epic, there is, as is usually the case with his critical strictures, a core of serious truth qualified by irony; the reader is offered excellent guidance which he must follow with caution because of a lurking suspicion that the deft hand of the narrator, in the midst of explanatory gestures, is somehow pulling his leg. The very presence of such prefaces, to begin with, should serve to remind us that Fielding is the first of the great intellectual novelists (whose procedures and allegiances, incidentally, do not wholly jibe with the standard definition of the novel as a bourgeois genre): like Flaubert, Joyce, James, Gide, he is anxious to define the novel in terms of literary tradition, modern and classical, and, like them, he theorizes about what he writes as he writes it. Fielding's association of the novel with the epic is suggestive in several ways, but what is most relevant to our present purpose is the implied assumptions about the function of language and the relationship of the writer to his audience.

A good deal has been said in recent years about the novel as private experience: the living-out of fantasy, which is of course essentially private, is usually thought of as the characteristic act of novel reading. But this surely does not account for our total experience as readers of novels, and Fielding, with a neoclassical conception of the epic very much in mind, repeatedly insists that a novel is something to be shared by a community of the discriminating. The force of the very first sentence in *Tom Jones*, which introduces the metaphor of the feast that will be sustained throughout the novel, is to make clear at once that the novel is conceived as public experience: "An author ought to consider himself, not as a gentleman who gives a private or eleemosynary treat, but rather as one who keeps a public ordinary, at which all persons are welcome for their money."

Now, the most public aspect of a literary work is its language, for words we all share in common, while the kinds of imaginings to which words stir us inevitably take place in the privacy of the individual mind, whatever hidden lines one believes there may be that connect individual minds to a superpersonal network of the collective unconscious. And it seems to me that the most fundamental influence of the epic on Fielding is in his decision to base the novel on the artfully ostentatious manipulation of words. In keeping with the general function of rhythmic beat, extended simile, formulaic recurrence in the epic, his most essential procedure as a novelist is constantly to enrich his fictional world by reminding us in different ways of the literary artifice through which that world comes into being. The most obtrusive expression of this tendency in his writing is, of course, his parodies of epic devices. Most of these, though ingenious enough, are far from representing an imaginative assimilation of the epic: the great mock-epic set pieces, like Molly Seagrim's churchyard brawl or Joseph Andrews' battle with the hunting dogs, are brilliant entertainments, not novelistic revelations. Of much more significance to Fielding's achievement as a creator of the novel is his success in fashioning a stylized language which, through the fine control of tone, rhythm, imagery, syntax, by the shrewd play with and against the received meanings of words, achieves the qualities of precision of reference, complexity of statement, aesthetically pleasing form, that are traditionally associated with the language of poetry.

Reading Fielding, and even more, rereading Fielding, we are repeatedly made aware of the way he maneuvers us into seeing characters, actions, values, society at large, from exactly the angle of vision he wants. The famous moment in *Tom Jones* when the philosopher Square is discovered behind the arras in Molly Seagrim's bedroom offers a kind of paradigm for Fielding's general method. The rug nailed over Molly's makeshift closet falls just as she is berating Tom for his infidelity, and the contents of the closet are suddenly revealed:

> where among other female utensils appeared—(with shame I write it, and with sorrow will it be read)—the philosopher Square, in a posture (for the place would not near admit his standing upright) as ridiculous as can possibly be conceived.
>
> The posture, indeed, in which he stood, was not greatly unlike that of a soldier who is tied neck and heels; or rather resembling the attitude in which we often see fellows in the public streets of London, who are not suffering but deserving punishment by so standing. (V, 5)

The phrase here that has often, and understandably, evoked comment is, of course, "among other female utensils." It is a miracle of satiric compression: the addition of that lethal "other" places Square for us precisely where Fielding wants him, reducing the teacher of noble ethical ideals to a kind of ambulatory dildo, heaped together with sundry unnamed female appurtenances which, as Molly's intimate possessions, would in all likelihood be neither very clean nor sweet nor pleasant to behold. The satiric point of the phrase, moreover, transfixes Molly together with Square, because the application here of "female utensils" brilliantly exposes the crude standard of sexual utilitarianism upon which she bases her relationships with men, Tom included. Having demolished his target, Fielding now circles back upon it with a more rhetorically oblique method of attack; just such shifts in strategy typify the general pattern of his shrewdly maneuvered prose. The narration pauses for a moment over the physical posture of the philosopher—the contorted figure of a man whose name and motto of "right rule of reason" imply geometrical rectitude—and then goes on to offer two detailed similes, ostensibly in order to help us visualize Square's awkward position. But the real function of the similes, clearly, is to contaminate the already exposed image of Square through association with the scurrilous objects of comparison: and so his posture is likened to that of a trussed-up soldier being punished for moral dereliction, and to the shameless squat of the London rabble in the act of using the streets as a privy.[1]

Throughout Fielding, similes are employed in a similar way, not merely as parodies of the extended epic simile, but as instruments to wrest from us, through the pressure of rhetorical persistence, a kind of comic assent to the writer's satiric judgments. With the most elaborate mock-solemnity, lawyers are carefully compared to butchers and hangmen, gossips to dove-rending kites, mercenary fathers of marriageable daughters to heartless bawds selling maidenheads to the highest bidder, and so forth.

The passage we have been considering illustrates one aspect of Fielding's prose which needs more emphasis than it has generally received. Because of the various prefatory materials, the constant authorial asides, the leisurely elaboration of figures of speech, one naturally thinks of Fielding as an expan-

sive writer, but there is a systole as well as a diastole in the
movement of his prose, and his apparently easy manner can
arrive suddenly at the most remarkable concentration of expression. When, for example, he comments in *Joseph Andrews*
on the surprisingly gracious reception of Pamela by Lady
Booby, his explanation is a complete essay in social criticism
in twelve innocent-looking words—"for she was perfectly
polite, nor had any vice inconsistent with good-breeding" (IV,
4). One can see at moments like this why the conventional
distinction between essayistic and novelistic passages in Fielding's fiction is essentially false. The social criticism here has
resonance because it reverberates against the actions and
passions of Lady Booby, whom we have seen in all her towering sexual egotism and relentless sexual hypocrisy both as a
realized character in a novel and as the representative of a
particular social code. Presentation of character and social
commentary are so nicely interwoven that it would be foolish
to try to separate them. There is, moreover, no real difference
in kind between this concise observation on the morals of
Lady Booby and the longer passages usually thought of as
"digressions" in Fielding. The point is that the moral and social commentator, Fielding the so-called essayist, is always
present: often he makes his presence felt, as here, by the
briefest passing reflection, or by the mere choice of an adjec-
tive or the position of a verb; at times he moves gracefully
through long and elaborate comic glissades from the particular to the universal and back again;[2] but the narrative
is everywhere one weave, steadily editorializing, sometimes
conspicuously, sometimes unobtrusively.

In regard to the capacity for concentrated statement of
Fielding's prose, it is of course the unobtrusiveness that needs
to be observed. Fielding himself warns us in *Tom Jones* that
the reader must be constantly on the alert if he is to read
the novel with pleasure and profit: "we shall not indulge thy
laziness where nothing but thy own attention is required;

for thou art highly mistaken if thou dost imagine that we intended, when we began this great work, to leave thy sagacity nothing to do" (XI, 9). As in a proper reading of Pope's couplets, a prehensile activity of the mind is called for, not only to seize on slippery hints about characters and plot and the application of veiled allusions, but also to catch the quick thrust of satirical wit in a phrase whose suddenness or obliquity scarcely gives us opportunity to take in its pointed meaning. It is easy for a reader to sail right past the epigram on Lady Booby without seeing the flash of its satire, or to miss, through sheer swiftness, the sharply ironic contradiction of the phrases that describe how the falsely accused Partridge "left the country, where he was in danger of starving, with the universal compassion of all his neighbours" (*Tom Jones*, II, 6).

The reader is also frequently required to attend not only to what the words say but to how they are arranged if he is to perceive the latent meaning of every statement. The main point, for example, in Fielding's report of the demise of Sir Thomas Booby is communicated through a finesse of syntax: "'At this time, an accident happened which put a stop to those agreeable walks [of Joseph's and Lady Booby's], which probably would have soon puffed up the cheeks of Fame, and caused her to blow her brazen trumpet through the town; and this was no other than the death of Sir Thomas Booby, who, departing this life, left his disconsolate lady confined to her house, as closely as if she herself had been attacked by some violent disease" (*Joseph Andrews*, I, 5). The sentence nicely illustrates why, from Fielding's point of view, there are better things to be done with language than to go poking around in people's minds. The finely controlled movement of revelation and the facetiously orotund use of the stock allegorical figure for fame are obviously the work of a self-conscious narrator. Nevertheless, the sentence, without actually imitating the processes of Lady Booby's consciousness, does mirror in its formal arrangement the distorted pattern of her values. The first mention of that regrettable accident, death, is almost buried under a series of introductory clauses, which, appropriately, are mainly devoted to apprehensions of possible harm to Lady Booby's reputation; and then the sentence moves on at once to the lamentable confinement of the new widow, sliding through Sir Thomas' death in a mere participial phrase and thus reducing it—as indeed it is reduced in Lady Booby's perspective of polite self-centeredness—to a kind of social inadvertency: the husband leaves his lady, "departing this life," as a man might be described forgetting his hat.

Prehensile activity of the mind is most especially and continually required for the reader to seize upon Fielding's coy ironies in the abundant variety of disguises under which they hide. It is, moreover, through his use of irony that Fielding most effectively focuses the moral meanings of his fiction by directing our attention to the language which conveys his imagined world to us. Language, as Fielding understands it and works with it, is both the necessary instrument for any moral analysis and one of the principal means through which we justify our institutionalized hypocrisies, deceive others and ourselves as well. Fielding's ironic strategies are marvelously various, but his most typical procedure is to order a statement in such a way that the awareness of its ironic counter-meaning gradually dawns on us, throwing a retrospective light on key words or phrases in the sentence to illuminate the falseness of their conventional application: we read forward, to find out what is happening, and, so to speak, backward, re-examining the tools of communication that belong to both the literary medium and the moral world we ourselves inhabit. Thus Fielding explains why Dr. Blifil, who has the misfortune to be married, does not even think of "criminal indulgences" with Bridget Allworthy: "This was owing either to his religion, as is most probable, or to the purity of his passion,

which was fixed on those things which matrimony only, and
not criminal correspondence, could put him in possession of,
or could give him any title to" (I, 10). By the time we arrive
at the double insistence on the rights of property at the end,
we realize that "purity" has been used in a chemical, not a
moral, sense—that is, unadulterated, suffering no admixture—
and, as the mock-morality of Dr. Blifil's motives is laid bare,
we begin to wonder whether marriage for gain as he coldly
conceives it might not be the most "criminal correspondence"
of all. Certainly, Bridget's liaison with the young Summer,
about which we learn much later, seems innocent by comparison.

Sentence after sentence in Fielding's fiction proves to be,
on the backward glance of reconsideration, a series of words
and phrases in hidden quotation marks, the decorous terminology that polite society uses to mask its dishonesties—"innocent freedoms," "matrimonial charms," "people of fashion,"
"virtue," "honour," "love," and many, many more. Such employment of language as an instrument of moral obfuscation
has obviously increased to the most threatening proportions in
our own time, but there is one important respect in which
Fielding's critical re-examination of moral vocabulary is predi-
cated on a linguistic situation that no longer obtains. Like many
of the major writers of prose and verse in eighteenth-century
England, he is able to assume a remarkable degree of fixed,
precise meaning for moral abstractions, largely because he
still has a sense that he is addressing himself to a known
audience which more or less shares with him a common
education and a particular set of social experiences. We can
see this assurance in use of terms in his conclusion to the
memorable disquisition on "high" and "low" people in *Joseph
Andrews:* "And yet there are scarce two of these who do
not think the least familiarity with the persons below them
a condescension and, if they were to go one step farther, a
degradation" (II, 13). The two strategic nouns here are em-

ployed almost as though they measured distances on a calibrated scale. Although the social situation being described is in fact one in which there is a good deal of upward mobility —and therefore snobbery—the terms used derive from a fixed social hierarchy where their meanings could be most precise because they referred to accepted, or objective, relationships, not to subjective attitudes.

The typical rhetorical strength built on this definiteness of verbal reference by English writers, from Addison to Jane Austen, is in firmness and efficiency of assertion. Fielding, on the other hand, more often develops strategies to call the received usage into question, revealing to his readers the untidy clutter of ambiguities, equivocations, and needed qualifications which have been swept under the neat rug of a supposedly assured term. This procedure is clearest in his use of verbal motifs in his novels. Probably the most sustained of these is the concept of "prudence" in *Tom Jones;* since the ironic treatment of this particular value has been studied intelligently and at length by Eleanor N. Hutchens,[3] I shall say only a few words about it to illustrate how Fielding's method operates to qualify conventional moral terms. Prudence is of course the great lesson Tom Jones must learn, but what happens to that word in the novel gives evidence of Fielding's dialectical approach to moral issues, even where he has been thought to be most didactic. If Tom's progress to maturity begins and ends with a solemn sermon by Squire Allworthy on the importance of prudence, sermons of a much more dubious nature, which also insist on prudence, are delivered during the course of the narrative by the formidable Aunt Western and the wayward Mrs. Fitzpatrick. Early in the book, Allworthy describes prudence to Tom as the "outward ornament" of virtue, but in the world of the novel the usual practice is to substitute the outward ornament entirely for the inward condition. The "prudent" people in the book are Mrs. Wilkins, Bridget, Blifil, Square and Thwackum, even Lady

Bellaston. The most casual satiric asides are used to raise further questions about the prudence of respectable society, like this comment on Tom's state after he realizes Sophia has discovered his infidelity with Mrs. Waters—"he being . . . in that situation in which prudent people usually desist from inquiring any further after their friends, lest they should be shocked by hearing such friends had hanged themselves" (XII, 3).

The apparent contradiction between the positive and negative meaning of prudence suggests something of the novel's large moral design: Fielding recognized that prudence, whose value he tried to teach, inevitably involved an element of calculation, while the ability to live the good life, as he conceived it, implied a capacity for spontaneous feeling and action which he knew might not be entirely compatible with the secondary virtue of prudence. His rich awareness of this threat of contradiction is embodied in his dialectical use of the term, in his repeated testing of the meanings of the word against the action of the novel.

Irony, according to an aphorism of Friedrich Schlegel, is the analysis of thesis and antithesis, and few novelists have illustrated the applicability of that definition so happily as Fielding. Moreover, this very process of dialectic analysis, as I shall try to show later, is the essence of Fielding's method in developing and deploying his characters, in articulating his themes, in planning the large structural units of his novels. On the level of style, irony operates upon the reader not only to make him aware of mutually qualifying meanings, but also to implicate him in a particular relationship with the narrator and the material narrated, and this relationship is important both in winning his assent to the values affirmed through the novel and in engaging his sympathetic appreciation for the kind of literary enterprise that is being undertaken.

For Fielding, despite the obvious relish with which he re-created contemporary English life, had to regard the novel from his traditionalist viewpoint as a kind of compromise—much the way Pope adopted the exquisitely witty mock-heroic mode of *The Rape of the Lock* as a blessed compromise for the English heroic poem he would never write—and irony provided the perfect means for effecting this compromise harmoniously. (Mixed feelings about the genre, it should be added, do not merely reflect Fielding's role as an initiator but constitute something like a generic undertone among novelists. A good many of them have wondered about the legitimacy of the genre in which they worked; some of the most venturesome, from Sterne to Beckett, have attempted to break down its limits or radically transform it from within.)

Irony, as we are often reminded, implies both complicity and superiority—complicity between the ironist and the discerner of the irony, who share a sense of intelligent superiority to the unwitting objects of the irony, or to any hypothetical persons who would take the ironic assertions at face value. The ironic attitude boosts Fielding, and his readers with him, to a firm position of elevation over the world he describes, and while few writers since have wanted to rise to such Olympian heights, some of the greatest novelists—Cervantes, Jane Austen, Flaubert, Joyce—have resembled Fielding in maintaining a careful ironic distance between them and the life they recorded. The perspective of irony is invaluable to the novel because of a danger inherent in the basic impulse of the genre to immerse us in contemporary reality; for reality seen from so close is likely to be a shapeless mass of clamorous particulars which can easily subvert both moral intelligence and aesthetic lucidity. This is clearly one of the bases for Fielding's objection to the whole method of *Pamela,* for his repeated insistence, *contra* Richardson, that a novelist must exercise the highest degree of selectivity and the finest narrative tact.

Irony, then, is used by the narrators of *Joseph Andrews*

and *Tom Jones* to establish for the reader an attitude toward the worlds of those novels which is both minutely attentive and coolly withdrawn. Fielding embraces the contemporary world with the delight of one who has re-created it lovingly, and yet his view of it remains oddly concessive—just as he is concessive in using the formula "in vulgar language" or "in plain English" when he begins, grudgingly, to translate one of his high-flying periphrases into the ordinary speech of mere groundlings. Because through irony Fielding can simultaneously engage the world of immediate experience and imply its moral and aesthetic inadequacy, his irony is inseparable from the meticulously preserved decorum of his style: they work together to control with nice precision how we are to think and feel about his fictional events.

The quality of archness that characterizes so many of his statements is especially relevant in this connection. Though his sly ingenuity may occasionally seem a bit self-admiring, it almost always has the effect of affirming an underlying moral-aesthetic viewpoint, as, for example, in his ambiguous account of Bridget Allworthy's attraction to Captain Blifil: "Though Miss Bridget was a woman of the greatest delicacy of taste, yet such were the charms of the captain's conversation, that she totally overlooked the defects of his person. She imagined, and perhaps very wisely, that she should enjoy more agreeable minutes with the captain than with a much prettier fellow; and forewent the consideration of pleasing her eyes, in order to procure herself much more solid satisfaction" (I, 11). The way the passage turns back upon itself ironically is clear: when we come to the final procurement of "solid satisfaction," our hovering suspicion about earlier phrases is fully confirmed; we realize that "delicacy" has been used in its older sense of "addiction to sensuous pleasures," that the captain's conversation is carnal, not verbal (as in the usage frequent in the eighteenth century, "criminal conversation"), and that Bridget's enjoyment with the captain is a matter of "agreeable minutes" rather than hours for practical reasons. Fielding goes on to supply a corresponding sexual innuendo for Captain Blifil's view of his obligations to Bridget, and later (II, 2), in order to assure us that we have not mistaken his meaning, he announces that "by reason of a fright" Bridget gave birth to a son eight months after the marriage ceremony.

It is worth considering for a moment what Fielding gains by reporting this relationship in such an archly oblique manner. It is obvious that other methods of narration here might be far more vivid and dramatic. A writer in the naturalist tradition could give us Bridget's quickened breath and sweaty palms, the grotesque coquetry of her amorous leer, the way she would sidle up to the captain, brushing her heavy flesh against him, and, finally, the two aging, graceless bodies shuddering together in furtive pleasure. Or, a novelist interested in rendering consciousness would reproduce Bridget's mental excitement, her kinesthetic response to the potent maleness of Captain Blifil's presence, catching us up in the tide of eagerness after frustration of a spinster who has tasted pleasure once, but, since the death of her lover over a year earlier, has been forced to live in arid celibacy. But a reader with such expectations, as Fielding dryly observes in justifying the omission of details about those most "ordinary occurrences" between Tom and Lady Bellaston, "is one whose devotion to the fair sex, like that of the papists to their saints, wants to be raised by the help of pictures" (XIII, 9).

Fielding's decorous reticence is clearly not the result of any personal inclination to prudery—we need only recall in this connection his hilarious allusions in *Shamela* to the size, function, and vulnerability of the sexual organs. On the contrary, the attitude communicated through his oblique manner is a sly knowingness about sexual matters. You and I, the narrator suggests to the reader through his irony and his stylistic decorum, are both men of the world who know what it's all about and who certainly understand what a frustrated spinster is really after; but we are, after all, cultured people who should therefore observe the proprieties of literature; we can apprehend the world and judge it without descending in our discourse to the level of its acts and words—*verba sapien-tiae* etc. The moral facts of real life, however sordid, are recognized and encompassed—and, of course, made immensely amusing—by this method of presentation, while the unseemly rawness of experience is carefully distanced: we are invited to infer its pungency without tasting it directly.

Paradoxically, Fielding's decision to avoid the grossness of exhaustive realism generates in his novels another kind of realism, which is essentially social and moral in nature. To bring us any closer to the undercover activities of Bridget and her lusty captain would be to take advantage of the special literary privilege of voyeurism, which, admittedly, is a favorite perspective of novelists from Richardson on. Fielding, however, is not at all interested in the affective side of the lovers' relationship but rather in what the relationship reveals about the nature of man, conceived in Augustan terms morally not psychologically, living in society. We discover the fact of Bridget's premarital indulgence much the way we would if we really lived in the community to which she belongs— through a process of alert inference, initiated by a predisposi-tion to suspicion to which Fielding's prose has rhetorically conditioned us, just as society morally conditions its members to cast a cold eye of suspicion on one another. Baldly stated, Bridget's carnal weakness would be a mere crudity or an uninteresting commonplace; but as Fielding makes us infer it, the bare fact hides teasingly behind a veil of innuendo, and innuendo of course implies attitude, bearing with it a sort of hovering moral judgment, potentially emphatic, yet not quite proper to be expressed. The realism of this whole pro-cedure, it should be stressed, is not in any "reproduction" of reality but in the creation through language of a process both analogous and aesthetically superior to one we live out in reality: we pick up Fielding's innuendo through the discrimination of verbal ambiguities in a beautifully wrought stylistic structure, not from the knowing smirk and tattletale whisper of gossip.

One briefer example should show still more clearly how authorial archness and stylistic decorum are manipulated to place us in just the relation to the novel that the writer wants. At two points in *Tom Jones*, Fielding introduces a discreet but strategic hint that, while Tom is out in the bushes tumbling his wench, young Blifil may be off in the woodshed, gratifying his desires with the aid of his own right hand: "The charms of Sophia had not made the least impression on Blifil; not that his heart was pre-engaged; neither was he totally insensible of beauty, or had any aversion to women; but his appetites were by nature so moderate that he was able, by philosophy, or by study, or by some other method, easily to subdue them" (VI, 4, and compare X, 9, last paragraph). Fielding's concessive realism is brilliantly effective here. Unlike Joyce, who could make out of the poetic description of an act of onanism one of the tours de force of the modern novel, Fielding has aesthetic misgivings as to whether this kind of reality belongs in serious literature. But from his perspective of moral realist, he squarely accepts it as a common human act we all know about and therefore as a distinctly possible act in the world of his novel. By merely hinting at it, however, with such sly indirection, he implicates us in his assumptions of taste and morals and casts over Blifil a darkening shadow of innuendo; what is communicated is not the "objective fact" that Blifil masturbates, but the powerful suspicion that he does, accompanied by the feeling, "Yes, and what a sneaking, mean-spirited, dirty little act it is!"

From all this, it ought to be apparent why in *Joseph Andrews* and, to a much greater degree, in *Tom Jones*, Fielding uses a self-dramatizing narrator who in a sense is, as some readers have suggested, his most fully realized character.[4] Since his whole literary method works on the tacit assumption of a community of values, both moral and aesthetic, between writer and reader—like that which united the epic poet and his audience—it is logical that he should reinforce this shared outlook by speaking through a witty, humane persona with whom we can feel a sort of urbane camaraderie of like intelligences. Or perhaps it might be more precise to say that he creates rather than reinforces shared outlooks, for Fielding is clearly aware that in his age the community of values, like the community of men, has lost much of the wholeness it may once have had—this is, from one point of view, why he must write comic-epic novels and not serious epic poems. He proceeds in his novels not only by affirming accepted values but also, as we have seen, by qualifying or even redefining some of them, as he redefines in *Tom Jones* the whole traditional literary idea of the hero. Through the creation of a narrator whom we come to like and trust, he is able to conjure up a sense of common viewpoint with the reader that is part actual persuasion, part fictional equivalent of real agreement. His success in this effort is one reason why so little in his two comic novels has dated despite all the obvious and intricate ways in which his writing is anchored in his period. We may no longer all think of masturbation as the unmitigated nastiness Fielding may have assumed his readers would judge it to be, but that hardly matters: the rhetorical strategy through which he suggests Blifil's manner of satisfying his "passion" makes us concur in the narrator's view of the act with an eager sympathy that is more than the willing suspension of disbelief.

To elicit this special quality of credence in the narrator from readers whose own world has increasingly little to be credited, Fielding repeatedly calls attention to his narrator's ironic self-awareness; we more readily believe the assertions of the "historian" because he frequently shows us how conscious he is of their potential absurdity. The strategies he adopts are obvious enough though always wittily employed. He introduces a stylistic flight to the sublime as "some very fine writing" (*Joseph Andrews*, I, 8); he disparages the erudition of "the author" in a footnote (*Joseph Andrews*, III, 3); he declines invoking the Muse at the end of a mock-epic passage "as she hath so lately been violently sweated" (*Tom Jones*, IV, 8); he threatens to "pour forth a vast profusion of learning" but, out of solicitude for the poor reader, thinks better of it (*Tom Jones*, V, 10). As the central expression of this self-irony, his whole treatment of the high style demonstrates the fine adjustment he manages to achieve between the claims of crude experience and those of elegant art. Some of his pretended elegances are simply broad burlesques, used to demonstrate the decidedly unheroic nature of contemporary reality through the verbal gymnastics of a pseudo-heroic language. But at times Fielding succeeds in having it both ways with his high style, which genuinely elevates its objects while hinting at the absurdity of the elevation. One memorable example of this double effect of style is the grand introduction of Sophia Western (IV, 1 and 2).

The heading for Book IV, "Containing the Time of a Year," is the first of the series of book headings devoted solely to the indication of length of time transpired. Immediately against it is set the heading for Chapter I, "Containing Five Pages of Paper," which directs our attention to the purely artificial medium of written words through which fictional life (the "time of a year" in the lives of Sophia and Tom) is transmitted. In keeping with this initial contrast, the whole operatic entrance of Sophia will be pointed with piquant juxtapositions of life and art. Thus the prefatory essay on the need for "poetical embellishments" in lengthy works is at most half-serious, and the narrator's manner here of inviting us into his cluttered workshop is a little reminiscent of Swift's Grub-Street Hack, that most egregious modern writer who is the supposed author of *A Tale of a Tub*. By anecdote and example, Fielding likens the need for interludes of the sublime in long narratives to the contemporary theatrical practice of introducing the hero with "a flourish of drums and trumpets" that will accommodate the ears of the audience to the "bombast and fustian" to be mouthed by the hero. Altering the simile, he remarks that at public processions, where the ancients would have had a priestess impersonating the real presence of the goddess Flora to strew flowers, we moderns must make do with a very mortal basket-woman for the same ceremonial task.

The "Short Hint of What We Can Do in the Sublime" which is the substance of the next chapter is precisely this—rhetorical flowers strewn by a transparently human basket-woman zestfully masquerading as a goddess. If Aeolus is immediately invoked, it is as "the heathen ruler of the winds," that is, as a god in whom we no longer really believe; if Eurus is grandly conjured to silence, his "sharp-pointed nose" gives him a suspiciously Hogarthian look. The soaring bard prepares in this way to swoop down after two paragraphs from the heights of Olympus to the toasts of the once fashionable Kit-cat Club and the pictures of the Hampton Court gallery, to a rude rejoinder of the famous Lord Rochester,[5] and then back upward to recount the passing loveliness of the fair Sophia. I think it misses the point to say that Sophia "never wholly recovers"[6] from all this introduction. The elevated style is honestly meant to give her a certain real grandness—and I think that it clearly succeeds—while the whole procedure is finely qualified by the continuous ironic awareness that we no longer believe in the traditional sublimities and that any language appropriate to them, if not completely discredited, is at least no longer entirely credible.

Fielding can do more than this with his ironic high style. He can use it to evoke a lofty mood and lyric setting, quickly modulate to parody, inflate his diction to patently unnatural proportions that reveal a satiric intention, and then explode the whole diaphanous bubble in a burst of earthy realism. The method illustrates itself much better than it can be summarized, so I shall quote at length, for here length is essential, a passage that is, justifiably, one of the most famous in *Tom Jones* —the description of Tom's topple from an apostrophe to Sophia into the outstretched arms of Molly Seagrim.

It was now a pleasant evening in the latter end of June, when our hero was walking in a most delicious grove, where the gentle breezes fanning the leaves, together with the sweet trilling of a murmuring stream, and the melodious notes of nightingales, formed all together the most enchanting harmony. In this scene, so sweetly accommodated to love, he meditated on his dear Sophia. While his wanton fancy roamed unbounded over all her beauties, and his lively imagination painted the charming maid in various ravishing forms, his warm heart melted with tenderness; and at length, throwing himself on the ground, by the side of a gently murmuring brook, he broke forth into the following ejaculation:

"O Sophia, would Heaven give thee to my arms, how blest would be my condition! Curst be that fortune which sets a distance between us. Was I but possessed of thee, one only suit of rags thy whole estate, is there a man on earth whom I would envy! How contemptible would the brightest Circassian beauty, dressed in all the jewels of the Indies, appear to my eyes! But why do I mention another woman? Could I think my eyes capable of looking at any other with tenderness, these hands should tear them from my head. No, my Sophia, if cruel fortune separates us for ever, my soul shall dote on thee alone. The chastest constancy will I ever preserve to thy image. Though I should never have possession of thy charming person, still shalt thou alone have possession of my thoughts, my love, my soul. Oh! my fond heart is so wrapped in that tender bosom, that the brightest beauties would for me have no charms, nor would a hermit be colder in their embraces. Sophia, Sophia alone shall be mine. What raptures are in that name! I will engrave it on every tree."

At these words he started up, and beheld—not his Sophia—no, nor a Circassian maid richly and elegantly attired for the grand Signior's seraglio. No; without a gown, in a shift that was somewhat of the coarsest, and none of the cleanest, bedewed likewise with some odoriferous effluvia, the produce of the day's labour, with a pitchfork in her hand, Molly Seagrim approached. Our hero had his penknife in his hand, which he had drawn for the before-mentioned purpose of carving on the bark, when the girl, coming near him, cried out with a smile, "You don't intend to kill me, squire, I hope?" "Why should you think I would kill you?" answered Jones. "Nay," replied she, "after your cruel usage of me when I saw you last, killing me would, perhaps, be too great kindness for me to expect."

Here ensued a parley, which, as I do not think myself obliged to relate it, I shall omit. It is sufficient that it lasted a full quarter of an hour, at the conclusion of which they retired into the thickest part of the grove. (V, 10)

The initial paragraph suggests a pleasant sense of sweet pastoral harmony while making us quickly aware that it is a parody of bad pastoral poetry and worse prose: the scene in which the tenderhearted lover casts himself on the ground is composed of a catalog of poetic clichés very much like the ones Pope makes brilliant fun of in the *Essay on Criticism*—gentle breezes that fan delicious groves, murmuring streams, a wanton fancy roaming, the melodious notes of the nightingale. When Tom begins to apostrophize, the artificiality of the language is still further heightened. Tom's words all stress a magnificent and preposterous distance from the realities of his physical and psychological makeup and the actual world he inhabits: his language is full of formal poetic inversions, rhetorical subjunctives, hackneyed hyperboles ("one only suit of rags thy whole estate"); he even reaches out to the greatest geographic distance, for a Circassian maid wearing jewels of the Indies, in order to express his meaning. The Tom who speaks here is a parody of the conventional Petrarchan lover, down to the familiar resolution to inscribe the name of his beloved on every tree. At this point life intrudes on literature, as we move in half a dozen words from the Circassian beauty in the grand Signior's seraglio to a plain English actuality—Molly Seagrim's dirty shift, the first detail through which we learn of her presence. It should be noted, however, that Fielding, after his characteristic fashion, is careful not to plunge us all the way down into the pungent reality of country girls with moist armpits and eager thighs. Molly is elegantly "bedewed," not soaked, with sweat, which in turn is beautifully rarefied into "odoriferous effluvia." And as to her particular strategies of enticement and what begins to transpire in the bushes as a consequence, these are "ordinary occurrences" that we know all about and from which Fielding, as always, invites us gracefully to withdraw.

As an instance of Fielding's general method, it is important to observe that this entire passage, in varying ways, is stylized, not just the first half. For stylization is pervasive in Fielding's fiction and this is one of the reasons why it works so well: the whole world of his comic novels, though modeled on reality, is carefully stylized, not merely the language. In this respect, I am sure that Fielding was not only following the bent of his native genius but applying in new ways techniques he had learned in his years of writing for the theater. For obvious reasons, speech and action invented for the stage, especially the comic stage, tend to be heightened or exaggerated representations of reality, so contrived that the characteristic lines are sharper, more immediately self-revealing, than they could be in actual experience. Much of the action in both *Joseph Andrews* and *Tom Jones* has this quality of stylization, cutting contours that are manifestly bolder than life. A whole series of broadly comic actions comes to mind —the climactic chain of bedroom confusions at Lady Booby's in *Joseph Andrews,* the wild free-for-all at the Upton inn in *Tom Jones,* Squire Western's precipitous change from the chase for Sophia to a chase for a fox. Less obvious are the many small actions that, on examination, read like comic stage directions translated into the idiom of the novel—Beau Didapper, after sheathing his hanger at the end of an averted brawl with Joseph, taking out a pocket-glass to readjust his hair (*Joseph Andrews,* IV, 11); Honour, rhapsodizing about Jones and oblivious to her mistress' blushes because she is all the while mesmerized by the contemplation of her own features in a mirror (*Tom Jones,* IV, 14).

Fielding's dialogue is just as pervasively stylized. This is apparent in the language his characters speak, which shifts from self-parody to literary parody to formal comic soliloquy, and even when simulating the vividness of earthy speech, is an artful exaggeration rather than a transcription of it. (We shall have occasion later to consider examples of such stylized dialogue when we examine Fielding's treatment of character.) Equally important, what the characters say as well as how they say it is usually stylized; much of it is rather improbable by the standards of ordinary realism but comically revealing and perfectly right in context. Thus Lady Booby offers an impassioned plea for the impregnability of her virtue: " 'If I had ever discovered any wantonness, any lightness in my behaviour: if I had followed the example of some whom thou hast, I believe, seen, in allowing myself indecent liberties, even with a husband; but the dear man who is gone' (*here she began to sob*), 'was he alive again' (*then she produced tears*), 'could not upbraid me with any one act of tenderness or passion' " (IV, 6). In real life, of course, a wife who despised her husband and lusted after a serving-boy would never say this; Lady Booby's hypocrisy confesses itself with such splendidly lucid theatricality that it is entirely appropriate for Fielding to include actual stage directions, properly italicized.

Or again, Mrs. Deborah Wilkins' charitable comments on the infant Tom are what not the sharpest-tongued spinster, though her soul were as shriveled as a prune, could have actually said, but precisely because of their bold stylization, they provide a wonderful moment of comic illumination: "It goes against me to touch these mis-begotten wretches, whom

I don't look upon as my fellow-creatures. Faugh! how it stinks! It doth not smell like a Christian. If I might be so bold to give my advice, I would have it put in a basket, and sent out and laid at the church-warden's door. It is a good night, only a little rainy and windy; and if it was well wrapt up, and put in a warm basket, it is two to one but it lives till it is found in the morning" (I, 3).

A small but instructive indication of Fielding's conception of dialogue is the fact that, in both *Joseph Andrews* and *Tom Jones,* he on occasion uses direct quotation and indirect discourse indifferently. This is to say, he assumes that the "author," with his emphatic sense of cunningly artificial statement, is always speaking, whether we hear the voice of the narrator or a character, and so there is no more than a technical difference if the character speaks for himself in first person or if the narrator speaks for him in third person. When, for example, Mrs. Slipslop reprimands Parson Adams for saving Fanny from rape, the whole "dialogue" (Fielding himself uses the word) is reported in the third person, while her remarks have precisely the same kind of calculated improbability as those of Mrs. Wilkins: "she said, 'She thought him properer for the army than the clergy: that it did not become a clergyman to lay violent hands on anyone; that he should have rather prayed that she [Fanny] might be strengthened'" (II, 13).

There is, to be sure, a significant difference between stylization and mere exaggeration, but I am convinced that in all these aspects of Fielding's writing the category of stylization is properly applicable because in all of them one can discern the essential element of formal pattern, which at once attests to the shaping hand of the craftsman and, however partially, suggests the unifying conception of meaning and manner that underlies the whole work. The pattern is more beautifully and firmly elaborated in *Tom Jones* than in *Joseph Andrews,* though it is largely present in the earlier novel as well. Perhaps the most exhilarating experience in reading *Tom Jones*—especially for us in an age when so many unities are shattered, so many styles of art and life deliberately fragmented—is the sense communicated through the poised arabesques of style of a magisterial intelligence, supremely in command of the whole world it presents us. In Fielding, as in his great admirer, Gibbon, the periodic style serves as a kind of immanent metaphor of control; it continually reminds us of the writer's ability to hold the varied data of a complex reality in coherent and significant order. His periods, ironically eloquent and eloquently ironic, are often small replicas of the architectural form of the whole novel. Dorothy Van Ghent, in one of her perceptive parentheses, has aptly noted this particular effect of mirrored patterns: while discussing the complicated unity of structure of *Tom Jones,* she observes incidentally that "many of Fielding's sentences are complex little 'plots' in themselves, where the reader must follow a suspended subject through a functional ornament of complications—qualifying dependent clauses and prepositional phrases and eloquent pauses—to be the dramatic predication or denouement." [7]

Such intricately developed periodic sentences are paradigmatic, but not quite typical, of the repetition of pattern in *Tom Jones,* since the varied demands of a long narrative often require more constricted, less elaborate syntactical structures. What I think lies at the heart of the pattern in Fielding's prose, the recurrent element that works almost subliminally to remind us that everything in the novel is part of a unified world of artifice, is his endlessly varied reduction of so many of his materials to sharply antithetical structures whose members are held in tight balance against each other. Perhaps, if we were determined enough at psychological or moral conjecture, we could assign an explicit "meaning" to this design of balance, but it seems wiser to conclude simply that it is a bedrock of aesthetic preference for Fielding. Like many novelists after him, his aesthetic assumptions and his habits of patterning language seem to have been crucially influenced by the kind of poetry he admired, and the English poet par excellence for him was, inevitably, Alexander Pope. No one else who has written English could have demonstrated to Fielding so spectacularly the beauties of finely controlled, elastically varied balancing, or the power of sudden illumination generated by sharp antithesis. The *Second Moral Essay*, because its subject is the essentially contradictory nature of woman, puts such elements of balanced opposition, which are everywhere in Pope, into especially lively play. I quote the last lines of the character of Narcissa and the beginning of the following passage (lines 61-73):

> Why pique all mortals, yet affect a name?
> A fool to pleasure, and a slave to fame:
> Now deep in Taylor and the Book of Martyrs,
> Now drinking citron with his Grace and Chartres.
> Now Conscience chills her, and now Passion burns;
> And Atheism and Religion take their turns;
> A very Heathen in the carnal part,
> Yet still a sad, good Christian at her heart.
>   See Sin in State, majestically drunk,
> Proud as a Peeress, prouder as a Punk;
> Chaste to her Husband, frank to all beside,
> A teeming Mistress, but a barren Bride.

Because Fielding does not write under the high compression of heroic couplets, the wit of his antitheses never detonates so sharply or rapidly as that of Pope's sustained volleys. Nevertheless, I suspect he owes at least partly to his reading of Pope the predilection for balancing his statements in neat seesaw movements that raise mere contrast to strict causal relationships where, by a law of comic physics, one side must go up if the other goes down. This, for example, is the way he compares Squire Western and his sister: "as the brother never foresaw anything at a distance, but was most sagacious in immediately seeing everything the moment it happened, so the sister eternally foresaw at a distance, but was not so quick-sighted to objects before her eyes . . . and, indeed, both their several talents were excessive; for, as the sister often foresaw what never came to pass, so the brother often saw much more than was actually the truth" (X, 8). Fielding's fondness for neatly antithetical pairs of characters has often been noted, and the two Westerns are of course just such a pair; but the degree to which the same kind of antithesis shapes his whole style has not, I think, been sufficiently observed. It is the matrix of his prose not only at obvious moments like this one, when two characters are being compared, but also very often when the actions of a single character are reported.

Thus Fielding offers to explain why Mrs. Wilkins, after taking so much time to fix her hair upon receiving a midnight summons from Mr. Allworthy, is so terrified at the sight of him in his nightshirt: "It will not be wondered at that a creature who had so strict a regard to decency in her own person should be shocked at the least deviation from it in another" (I, 3). The concise antithesis both produces a witty neatness of formulation and teases us into thought. Mrs. Wilkins' two unrelated actions, one a result of her vanity, the other of her prudery, are bracketed together by rhetoric and set into seesaw motion on a fulcrum of specious causal logic. Or perhaps, we begin to wonder, the two actions are related, though not in the way the sentence pretends: Mrs. Wilkins before the mirror could conceivably have had vague expectations from being called at that hour to her master's bedroom which she would scarcely admit to herself, and her excessive shock at his dishabille might be a spinster's fears of what she unconsciously anticipates, or possibly, the result of a resolution to yield herself while preserving her reputation for virtue through the shrillest protestations of concern for it.

Antithesis, as should be evident from this instance, is used by Fielding not merely to give a pleasing symmetry to his style but to focus satiric meanings with a high degree of concentration. Nowhere is the satiric utility of this pervasive stylistic feature more vividly illustrated than in the chapter that reports the differing effects of Captain Blifil's death upon Squire Allworthy and Bridget (II, 9). From the expansively facetious chapter heading to the final words of Captain Blifil's epitaph, in which the widow designates "this stone" as "the monument of . . . her affection," Fielding clearly means to transform the episode of bereavement into farce, and antithesis is his principal instrument in the process of comic transformation. To begin with, he seats Bridget and her brother squarely at the opposite ends of his rhetorical seesaw, so that as one goes up, the other comes down; in this way voluntary actions assume mechanical regularity, people become puppets, in a perfect example of Bergsonian comedy. When the family realizes that Captain Blifil is missing, Squire Allworthy is so disturbed that, suppressing an urge to cry, he can barely speak; "but as grief operates variously on different minds, so the same apprehension which depressed his voice elevated that of Mrs. Blifil." The two characters are symmetrically "operated" upon by the same mechanical force, while our awareness of the merely rhetorical nature of this link between them leads us to contrast the spontaneity of Allworthy's response to the purely histrionic nature of Bridget's. The distraught wife, after an appropriate series of heartfelt ejaculations, begins to weep, and this transition is duly marked by a further antithesis: "Here a torrent of tears had the same consequence with what the suppression had occasioned to Mr. Allworthy, and she remained silent." At this point, Captain Blifil's body is brought on the scene, and Fielding announces the effects of that portentous event by swinging his seesaw to reversed positions: "Here the curious reader may observe another diversity in the operations of grief: for as Mr. Allworthy had been before silent, from the cause which had made his sister vociferous, so did the present sight, which drew tears from the gentleman, put an entire stop to those of the lady, who first gave a violent scream, and presently fell into a fit."

The symmetries of formulation now branch out in different directions. Two doctors, hastily summoned, and, for neatness of geometrical balance, referred to as Dr. Y. and Dr. Z., take positions on opposite sides of the body: one seizes its right arm, the other its left; one argues for apoplexy, the other for epilepsy. Seeing that the captain is no longer in need of their help, they proceed to lay hold on each of Bridget's hands, "as they had before done on those of the corpse"; and just as she was earlier bracketed antithetically with her brother, so she is now linked with her dead husband: "The case of the lady was in the other extreme from that of her husband: for as he was past all the assistance of physic, so in reality she required none." In this ingeniously symmetrical arrangement, the disconsolate widow, whose feelings are all strained artifice, is placed at a midpoint between Allworthy, who has the feelings of a real living person, and the inert captain, who is forevermore beyond all feeling.

From instances like this, one can see that Fielding belongs with the group of novelists which includes such varied figures as Sterne, Conrad, Proust, Joyce, and Faulkner, for whom style is not just the means of conveying or framing events but, often, the event itself. In this respect, the Osborne-Richardson film version of *Tom Jones* was faithful to the original in using silent black-and-white footage and comic subtitles at the beginning, in occasionally projecting a still shot, and in other ways making the manipulation of the medium itself generate some of the comedy.[8] At times Fielding seems almost to anticipate such cinematic comic techniques, as in his description of the dual between Tom and Fitzpatrick: "Jones . . . pressed on so boldly upon Fitzpatrick that he beat down his guard, and sheathed one half of his sword in the body of the said gentleman, who had no sooner received it than he stepped backwards, dropped the point of his sword, and leaning upon it, cried, 'I have satisfaction enough: I am a dead man'" (XVI, 10). The action itself here is not necessarily funny but the manner of its relation is hilarious. With a superb sense of comic timing, Fielding speeds up the pace of narration, much the way reducing the number of frames in filming turns natural movements into ridiculous stacatto jerks, and so we have Fitzpatrick, "the said gentleman," suddenly impaled on a sword, confessing, before we can quite finish blinking, that he has had satisfaction enough.

Moments such as this, however, are simply bright comic byplay. What is, finally, the most important function of Fielding's style, with its recurrence of antitheses and syntactical couplings, is the continually integrating activity brought about through it. Pretense is related to practice, one character to another, one act or posture to another which follows or to one in a completely different sphere of experience, the habits of the upper classes to those of the lower, country custom to city fashion, what goes on in England to the general state of the supposedly Christian nations. An intriguing aspect of the novel as a genre is that it has been driven from its inception by two opposite impulses—to explore the nature of private experience, which had been given a new and problematic importance by the changing social order, and to imagine the whole sweep of contemporary society, in a period when that was becoming progressively less imaginable. Fielding clearly belongs with those novelists who seek to evoke panorama, moral as well as social; he is attracted to the epic, in fact, partly because of its striking panoramic aspects, as Parson Adams' glowing praise of *opsis* in Homer (*Joseph Andrews*, III, 2) attests. But since Fielding's plots obviously represent a relatively limited selection of social possibilities and moral situations, it is chiefly through his integrating style that he achieves the artistic illusion of an all-encompassing vision of contemporary life. The activity of comprehensive integration, moreover, is basic to his whole conception of novel writing, and it will be essential for an understanding of both his attitude toward character and the larger structural unities of his fiction.

*A story based upon those elementary passions
in which alone we seek the true and final manifestation
of character must be told in a spirit of intellectual
superiority to those passions. That is, the author
must understand what he is talking about.*
—Henry James, review of Our Mutual Friend

3. THE DESIGN OF CHARACTER

The principal elements of a novel, as the critical common-place goes, are so organically interrelated that to talk about one is to imply all the others, but most readers of novels have quite naturally assumed the primacy of one particular element, often isolating it from the others for discussion. That element is, of course, character. At least for the average reader, and to a large extent for the sophisticated reader as well, novel reading, in general contrast to other kinds of reading, has chiefly meant living imaginatively with imaginary personages. There are few of us, whatever we think we know about style, structure, intellectual coherence, and the like, who do not judge a novel first of all by the degree to which its characters seem to us interesting, complex, consistent, likable, "real." *Tristram Shandy* was honestly enjoyed, even when its bold exploration of the limits of narrative form was ignored, for the touching and absurd goodheartedness of Uncle Toby and the splendidly pedantic quixotry of his brother Walter; and *Ulysses* remains more than an inexhaustible mine for dissertation topics because, through the convolutions of experiment in structure and style, a man emerges, Leopold Bloom, disarmingly pathetic, improbably heroic even in his failures, humanly large in his averageness, flesh of our flesh and bone of our bones.

But with all this obvious centrality of character in the experience of novel reading, we have as yet been given only partial and often less than cogent accounts of how character in the novel differs in kind from character in the older narrative genres or in drama. I do not pretend to offer here an adequate solution to this vastly complicated problem, but I would like to suggest briefly two broad possibilities of treating character that become more fully feasible because of the novel form.

It is often said that in the novel we get to know people with a degree of intimacy and completeness not possible in real life. Like all truisms, this needs some elaboration before it can be really informative. The privilege of perfect knowingness, to begin with, is shared in some degree by novelists with all literary creators of characters, who, by virtue of their role as creators, ideally can apprehend everything about their personages, however little they choose to reveal. We surely know Hamlet, and in a more limited way we know Odysseus or the David of the biblical cycle of stories, as we could never succeed in knowing flesh-and-blood men through the blocked and circuitous channels of our own experience. One difference between the privileged knowledge of the novel and that of other genres is in the contexts of the knowing: the novel reveals to us the essence of character in the trivial and the quotidian as well as in crisis and portentous act. We can know a character in a novel not only by the why and whether of his decision to commit suicide but also by the why and whether of his taking raspberry preserves with his toast—a kind of detail for which drama usually has no leisure and epic and romance little aesthetic tolerance. Leisureliness and an omnivorous appetite for details explain not only the differing contexts but also the distinctive quality of knowledge about character in the novel. We may know Lady Macbeth as intensely and lucidly as we do Emma Bovary, but never so intimately. It is in the novel, where the open and expansive narrative form allows the writer to reconstruct inner states minutely with words, that we can see a person from the vantage point he alone enjoys in real life, from behind his own eyes.

The sort of novel where we know characters through their own consciousness may conceivably be the prevailing tradition of the genre, but it would be a serious mistake to think of it as the only "authentic" kind of novel. If the novel's generic amplitude has encouraged some writers to penetrate character and re-create it from within, it has led writers of a different bent to walk around character, observe it minutely, make it come alive through the process of analytic description itself. There are, then, two kinds of knowledge of character which the novel form makes readily available—the empathetic knowledge of imaginative identification and the evaluative knowledge of discriminating observation: characters in novels may be invitingly permeable or beautifully perspicuous. Sometimes, one finds both modes of apprehension in a single novel, as in *Middlemarch,* where we are completely engaged in the life of Dorothea Brooke both by seeing events and people through her eyes and by watching George Eliot place her so precisely through abundant comment on her family, her social and cultural antecedents, her habits of thought and feeling, her actions.

Fielding is plainly a novelist wholly committed to perspicuity, not permeability, in the creation of character, and it is well to keep in mind from the outset that the refusal to render inner states is a conscious decision on his part, made from the awareness that entering into his personages would preclude precisely the kind of knowledge of character in which he is interested. As the narrator of *Tom Jones* tartly puts it, after declining at one point to reproduce Blifil's frustrated reflections, "It would be an ill office in us to pay a visit to the utmost recesses of his mind, as some scandalous people search into the most secret affairs of their friends, and often pry into their closets and cupboards, only to discover their poverty and meanness to the world" (IV, 3). Fielding is generally concerned with judgment, a fact attested to by the recurrent allusions and structural analogies in his two comic novels to actual trial procedure. Judgment requires distance from those to be judged, and Fielding is always careful to maintain it. In the sentence just quoted, to bring us any closer to Blifil would be to lose moral perspective on him, while the act of withdrawing from Blifil's consciousness is itself ingeniously used to pronounce a judgment: there are some cesspools, the narrator in effect says, whose bottoms we need not dredge in order to know all we could want to know about their contents. Fielding's procedure here is exactly the opposite of Richardson's in *Clarissa,* where author and readers share Lovelace's sensations as he presses his eye to the key-hole to watch the quiveringly vulnerable body of the captive Clarissa. Despite Richardson's moralistic intentions, the close identification with character loses all ethical reference, merely enabling writer and reader to share the lip-smacking pleasures of the novel's sadist-voyeur. It is of course possible to participate in the inner life of fictional characters without losing critical perspective, a fact abundantly demonstrated by the achievements of Flaubert, James, Tolstoi, and many other major novelists. There is, however, at least a threat to the preservation of judgment implicit in the novelist's imaginative identification with his characters; Richardson illustrates this point nicely because both his genius and his limitations are bound up in his uncanny ability to imagine himself into his personages.

We tend, I suspect, to be wary of the faculty of judgment, imagining that its continual exercise will somehow reduce characters, flatten and simplify them. In Fielding, for the most part, quite the reverse is true: his characters become more vividly alive, even more complex, as he judges them and asks us to judge them. This is especially surprising because his treatment of characters is not particularly analytical. When we read George Eliot, we are often prepared to believe that her personages are as many-sided as the people we know in actual experience—and much more lucidly perceived—because she talks all around them so intelligently. Fielding, on the other hand, not only takes a consistently external view of his characters but also makes little attempt to delineate their fine contours or fill in their subtle shadings as social and moral entities. It is not hard to see why critics have objected to the "superficiality" of his characterization. But if Fielding can break all the rules and nevertheless create characters who have managed to arrest the imaginations of so many readers in the course of two centuries, one may wonder whether the rules themselves are not too restricted.

The function served by analysis of character or impersonation of character in the work of other novelists is generally carried out in Fielding's fiction through integration of character —that is, the multiple strategies he adopts to relate individual characters to one another and to a large, coherent moral vision. Though Fielding is clearly much closer to the analytical novelists than to those whose first interest is consciousness, he typically uses the amplitude of the novel form not to walk around characters and closely observe their particularity but to step back from them and set them firmly in an embracing system of moral possibilities. Fielding the "essayist" is crucially important in this regard: as the nature and actions of his characters repeatedly lead him to expatiate on life, in his urbane and wittily knowing manner, we actually come to believe more fully in his characters and to understand them better. I realize that this assertion flies in the face of all our prejudices against novelists' talking at large, but I think an example will show that it corresponds more closely to most readers' experience of Fielding than they themselves would initially suspect.

Of the many secondary characters in *Tom Jones* who enjoy limited attention but abundant vitality, one of the most engaging is Tom's supposed mother and temporary bedmate, Jenny Jones. As with so much else in Fielding's handling of character, action, and style, a good part of our pleasure in contemplating Jenny comes from the delights of inferential activity: we are offered a series of hints and fragments of information about her which, pieced together, form an intriguing configuration of personality. Jenny is a plain girl whose physical attractions seem to be limited to buxom womanly health; something of a female intellectual (an aversion of Fielding's) with a keener appetite for men than for learning; an embodiment of anti-prudence in the novel, contemptuous enough of conventional opinion (or is it simply foolish enough?) to sell her reputation to Bridget Allworthy; admirably honest and loyal in her way, yet also capable of deception and amazingly facile in changing partners for her role as wife without benefit of clergy. In the often noted tripartite structure of the novel—six books in the country, six on the road, six in London—she occupies the pivotal position, being the Loose Woman of the road, as Molly Seagrim is of the country and Lady Bellaston is of the town. Her symmetrical role in the series of Tom's mistresses contributes to our sense of her character by way of comparison and contrast: she shares with Molly and Lady Bellaston an inflammable female concupiscence, but, over against Molly's crude and selfish contrivances with men and milady's citified corruption, she seems morally sound, as open (and unsafe) as the English roads with which she is associated. Jenny is moreover, a kind of structural linchpin for the novel as a whole: though she is Tom's mistress only in the central section on the road, she participates in the town and country sections as well, connected as she is both with the mysteries of Tom's birth in Somersetshire and the clarifications of the London denouement.

To a large extent, then, Fielding's shrewdly reticent presentation of details of characterization invites us to reconstruct character by inference, just as the cues for his verbal irony invite us to summon up a sustained alertness as readers in order to revise and reconstruct verbal meanings. All this makes Jenny Jones decidedly interesting though not exactly complex, certainly not as we expect characters to be complex in psychological novels. But, instead of a detailed "rendering" to make us believe in the autonomy of his characters, Fielding achieves the same result by respecting the individual characters' claims to be judged fairly yet rigorously, humanely, with wise consideration; and in this connection the so-called essayistic aspects of his writing are indispensable in helping to realize the characters. A more conventional eighteenth-century novelist—say, Smollett—would have turned the runaway Jenny into a slatternly camp follower, tracing the expected Harlot's Progress of the period; a Victorian might perhaps have sentimentalized her into a Fallen Woman, the innocent soul cruelly used by a cruel world. Fielding, however, maintains a fine balance in viewing Jenny and in directing our judgment of her, which is to say, he treats her as though she were a living person, not a conventional literary formula or a manipulable puppet.

Thus, when Jenny, after leaving one lover and then escaping the murderous hands of another, fixes her eager eye on Tom, Fielding explains, in his discursive manner, why she is not much troubled by the evident signs that Tom's affections are already engaged elsewhere:

The beauty of Jones highly charmed her eye; but as she could not see his heart, she gave herself no concern about it. She could feast heartily at the table of love, without reflecting that some other already had been, or hereafter might be, feasted with the same repast. A sentiment which, if it deals but little in refinements, deals however, much in substance; and is less capricious, and perhaps less ill-natured and selfish, than the desires of those females who can be contented enough to abstain from the possession of their lovers, provided they are sufficiently satisfied that no one else possesses them.

(IX, 6).

There is clearly no attempt here to reproduce Jenny's inner experience; the narrator is wholly concerned with clarifying and assessing her motives, with writing, if you will, a little moral essay on them. Yet in one respect the effect is the same as if he had actually represented her living through this moment. We feel he is taking her seriously as a person—and so he is able to imagine her with the kind of fullness that recognizes the lack of fastidiousness in her sexual urge and at the same time gives weight to the frankness and naturalness of her desire, especially as it compares with other kinds of sensuality and sexual egotism described or alluded to in the novel. Simple physical desire, for all the dangers to which it can lead, is a very human impulse, Fielding suggests, and can be a generous one as well: this is what finally redeems Tom's infidelities to Sophia, and it is the embodiment of this moral awareness in the characterization of Jenny Jones that makes her seem a credible flesh-and-blood woman, from her secret pact with Bridget to her countryside adventures and her final vindication of Tom. Thus the realism of "assessment" by which Ian Watt distinguishes Fielding from what he sees as the central tradition of the novel in fact generates a "realism of presentation" of its own.[1]

It should be noted, moreover, that the effect of Fielding's comments on Jenny here is to direct our attention outward toward the correlations of this particular judgment in the larger scheme of the novel. The invocation of the familiar metaphor of food for sex invites us to compare its application elsewhere in the novel: for Blifil, the prospect of sexual

gratification with Sophia is a kind of hideous gourmandizing
(VII, 6); for the generality of men, who mask their lust as
love, it is a glutton's desire for a juicy sirloin (VI, 1). Alongside these, Jenny's willingness simply to eat her full at a table
where others have been served seems healthy and honest.

The detailed psychological realization of character has been
assumed to be so basic to the novel that I think it is worth
considering further precisely how Fielding manages to get
along without it. There are times, to be sure, when his balanced judgment of characters comes to the brink of psychological analysis; what is to be learned, however, from such
moments is not that Fielding is an unfulfilled psychologist
but rather that generalized moral assessment can be an effective novelistic equivalent for particularized psychological
rendering. Take, for example, the moment in *Tom Jones* (VII,
9) when Sophia resolves to yield to her father's wishes and
marry Blifil. Fielding adduces filial affection and piety as her
motives, and then suggests an additional reason for her decision: "Lastly, when she reflected how much she herself was
to suffer, being indeed to become little less than a sacrifice,
or martyr, to filial love and duty, she felt an agreeable
tickling in a certain little passion, which though it bears no
immediate affinity either to religion or virtue, is often so kind
as to lend great assistance in executing the purposes of both."
One can see how much more dispassionately realistic Fielding
is in imagining his heroine than are the Victorian novelists in
creating that whole bevy of rosy-cheeked, lily-white maidens
whom Sophia, for some readers, has seemed to resemble. In
contrast, moreover, to Sophia's memorable counterpart in the
eighteenth-century novel, Clarissa, whose masochism is profoundly imagined but scarcely guessed at by her creator,
Fielding has all his heroine's emotions clearly in view, writing
about them, as Henry James would have wanted, "in a spirit
of intellectual superiority to those passions." Sophia is a perfectly healthy and altogether admirable young woman, but

Fielding knows quite well that even such a woman may nurture a hidden desire for self-immolation (or, alternately, for the pleasure of self-righteous grievance), and he catches just the right moral and psychological nuance for that desire by calling it, with no further specification, "an agreeable tickling in a certain little passion."

What ought to be noticed, however, is that this whole observation, which does such an efficient job in making a psychological discrimination, is undertaken from the moralist's viewpoint, is, in fact, quite as essayistic in perspective as any of the long "digressions" in Fielding. Such a perspective is manifest in the way the sentence is put together: we begin with what is going on inside Sophia ("when she reflected . . . she felt . . ."), but having arrived at that "certain little passion," the sentence swings out to a generalized consideration of the passion ("which though it bears . . . is often so kind . . .") and the way it encourages self-deception in all kinds of apparently well-meaning people.

Although the presentation of character is in one respect analytic here, its basic movement remains integrative, making Sophia real by relating her to others, explaining her motives in terms of a universal passion that may be seen operating —in this instance, by the narrator and his audience, not in the action of the novel—in very different persons, in circumstances perhaps similar or at least broadly analogous to Sophia's.

The treatment at this point of Sophia's mixed motives does not finally differ in kind from the presentation of Black George's conflicting motives (VI, 13, the last two paragraphs) in his decision not to appropriate the sixteen guineas Sophia has given him for Tom, as he has already appropriated Tom's £500 note. Black George's inner struggle is deliberately schematized into an allegorical debate between Conscience and Avarice which is resolved by the persuasive intervention of Fear. The aim of the amusing allegory, like that of the quasi-allegorical abstractions in English neoclassical poetry, is to elucidate and generalize the particular character's moral condition. Because of the breadth of Fielding's moral imagination, the individual Black George does not dwindle in this process of generalization: Fielding knows rascality well enough to see that it can exist perfectly well together with a kind of sneaking, timorous sense of decency, and that even so unscrupulous a fellow as Black George may care enough about the claims of honor to want to persuade himself that he has some scruples. The narrator is for once speaking with complete candor when in the next chapter he says that, from his vantage point "behind the scenes of this great theatre of Nature," he can censure George without absolutely detesting him. This is just the humanizing effect that Fielding's moral realism is meant to have on the reader: by seeing precisely what universal passions operate upon George, by comparing his treachery with that of the more malicious characters and observing the final role he plays in the novel, we can judge him rigorously without utter condemnation and even find him, in his clumsy, underhanded way, quite likable.

Just as the sustained process of moral evaluation in Fielding can function as an equivalent to psychological rendering, the closely related activity of irony also has the effect at times of making the characters seem more lifelike and complex. William Empson has written suggestively, if somewhat diffusely, on Fielding's "double irony" [2]—double because it incorporates a recognition of possible validity in the very positions it sets out to destroy. Now, when double irony is focused upon a character, it satirically exposes its target while sustaining an imagination of what it is like to be that person, with all his absurdities, pretensions, self-deceptions, or whatever the case may be. Irony, in order to be effective when directed against characters, must stay on the outside, but, paradoxically, such double irony offers us despite its externality a needle's-eye entrance—if we are nimble and not camel-like as readers—into character.

This will become clearer through example. At one point in *Tom Jones* (VII, 9), Fielding ironically adopts the viewpoint of Aunt Western, defending her "good nature" and "forgiving temper" by citing a recent adventure that befell her: "she had even broken the law, in refusing to prosecute a highwayman who had robbed her, not only of a sum of money, but of her earrings; at the same time d____ning her, and saying 'Such handsome B____s as you don't want jewels to set them off, and be d____n'd to you.'" The initial irony is quite simple—Mrs. Western's ostensible good nature in forgiving the highwayman is entirely the product of her flattered vanity. But this straightforward ironic reversal leads us into what is, in the proper sense of the word, an insight into the nature of the character. We see Sophia's spinster aunt in her pathetic aspect as an unattractive aging female, clinging quite desperately to the least hint of a compliment to her charms, no matter what the source; we see this, however, from an ironic distance, so there is no danger that our awareness of her pitiful state will spill over into sentimentality. At this point, if we begin to reflect on the highwayman's remark, the irony of Mrs. Western's delusions about her own "forgiving temper" redoubles: since all the evidence in the novel suggests that this "handsome b____h" deserves only the last half of the epithet, the highwayman's judgment should give us pause. Either his taste in women is badly defective or he is speaking sarcastically and means to say, "With a face like that, you're wasting your time wearing earrings." In either case, Mrs. Western's gratification over the compliment would be an even more painful case of self-deception than it first seemed.

Irony as Fielding uses it is more than a means of limited access to character; at least with some of his memorable comic figures, it seems to be his own way of imagining the character into life, the armature around which he has wound a unity of believable thought and speech and action. Ronald Paulson, in a brief but perceptive essay on Fielding, has made a very helpful suggestion about this connection between irony and the invention of character: "The ironic pose . . . may also create a kind of psychological verisimilitude when applied to character . . . Simple concession (accepting the opponent's point of view), fallacious argument, and high burlesque (both moral extensions of the enemy's own logic) are all moving in the direction of a dramatic imitation of the enemy—allowing him to speak for himself, or take himself at his own evaluation." [3]

When Lady Booby, in the first of the great seduction scenes in *Joseph Andrews* (I, 5), tries to lure Joseph to bed with a fluttering show of gentle fears and soft flesh, the dialogue is clearly based on this kind of ironic imitation, intended to expose the gap between her ladylike protestations of virtue and her thorough carnality. But Lady Booby is more than a satiric cartoon. Though some of the gestures and words assigned to her are patently stagey, the ironic conception which shapes her speech generally makes it the revealing expression of a proud and lustful woman. Fielding the ironist manages to capture the excitement with which she relishes her expected consummation with Joseph, her uneasiness about her reputation, her habitual facility in edging uncomfortable moral terms out of the way, her eager prurient anticipation of "submitting" herself to her own footboy, the mistress deliciously mastered by a servant:

"La!" says she, in an affected surprise, "what am I doing? I have trusted myself with a man alone, naked in bed; suppose you should have any wicked intentions upon my honour, how should I defend myself?" Joseph protested that he never had the least evil design against her. "No," says she, "perhaps you may not call your designs wicked; and perhaps they are not so."—He swore they were not. "You misunderstand me," says she; "I mean if they were against my honour, they may not be wicked; but the world calls them so. But then, say you, the world will never know anything of the matter; yet would not that be trusting to your secrecy? Must not my reputation be then in your power? Would you not then be my master?"

The effect Fielding achieves with Lady Booby, and with most of his comic characters, is a double one. She is, as I tried to show earlier, deliberately stylized, and so is entirely different in kind from the finely qualified and complicated haughty women of a novelist like Proust, or even Jane Austen. Yet the satiric simplification of the character's outlines by no means precludes a striking fidelity to psychological actualities in the characterization.

In the case of Lady Booby, this conjoining of satiric exaggeration and verisimilitude is splendidly illustrated in her confrontation with Parson Adams on the subject of Fanny and Joseph (IV, 2). The theatrical Lady Booby, whom we have observed before, is very much in evidence here, bristling higher and mightier than life, dismissing the clergyman at the end of the interview with a kind of magnificently proud pretense of virtue that reality is too lackluster to attempt: "I condemn my humility for demeaning myself to converse with you so long." The verbal keynote of the dialogue also looks like a theatrical device: Parson Adams naively tries to defend Fanny by calling her the most handsome woman, noble or otherwise, that has ever been seen in the parish; at this, Lady Booby begins to fulminate, returning again and again with furious sarcasm to Adams' mention of Fanny's "beauty." The mechanical repetition by a character of a single word or phrase is a familiar and amusing stage device for the revelation of comic rigidity, but it is more than that here. Parson Adams has unwittingly wounded Lady Booby in the most tender point of her sexual and social pride. A crude young country girl, with the smell of the dairyshed still clinging to her, has been named as the superior in beauty to an accomplished and universally admired lady who, alas, must fear the truth of the comparison because her enticements have been twice spurned by Joseph, while the desirable young man seems more than eager to accord Fanny what he refused Lady Booby. The lady's apprehensions about her own feminine charms and her envious resentment against her lowborn rival drive her to harp obsessively on the unequaled "beauty" Adams has ascribed to Fanny. Even after she has sent the parson away, that terrible word continues to rankle in her mind, and she spews it out again to Lawyer Scout (IV, 3), who offers her a sycophant's hollow consolation by answering with what they both know to be a lie, that Fanny is one of the ugliest creatures imaginable. There are obvious limits to the subtlety with which Fielding's noblewoman is presented, but at moments like this she seems not only comically grotesque but also terribly real.

The theatricality in Fielding's novels has often been noted, especially in its more obvious aspects which tend to weaken verisimilitude, but it needs to be stressed that Fielding's application of the devices of the theater is also frequently a means of making literature seem more, not less, lifelike. Of Fielding's recent critics, only Irvin Ehrenpreis, in his bright little book on *Tom Jones,* has demonstrated a full awareness that "life as a theater" has far more extensive implications for Fielding than the hoariness of the metaphor might lead one to suspect. A perceptive observation by Ehrenpreis on the interplay between artificiality and naturalness in *Tom Jones* aptly suggests the integral function of theatrical elements in Fielding's representation of life: "The constant dwelling on effects of spectacle and theatre seems an ironical consequence of Fielding's preoccupation with deceit and candour, affectation and simplicity, because the stage devices . . . remind one endlessly that art reveals the truth through seeming, while life misleads us through artfulness." [4] Theatricality has an important bearing on character as we perceive it in reality because so much of human experience, certainly from Fielding's point of view, is a matter of role playing. His generalization about men and masks in "An Essay on the Knowledge of the Characters of Men" could serve as a theoretical justification for the entire arrangement and presentation of characters—and almost a description of the plot, too—in both *Tom Jones* and *Joseph Andrews:* "Thus while the crafty and designing part of mankind, consulting only their own separate advantage, endeavor to maintain one constant imposition on others, the whole world becomes a vast masquerade, where the greatest part appear disguised under false vizors and habits; a very few only showing their own faces, who become, by so doing, the astonishment and ridicule of all the rest." [5]

Adopting an artificial role, moreover, is not merely the gesture of the deceiver whom the novelist conceives only to expose satirically. Fielding is able to imagine his way far enough into the more substantial of his role players to see that very often the role becomes a substitute for the man, the imposition upon others proving to be an imposition on self, too; so that in these cases, the acting out of a part begins to assume a significant aspect of psychological truth. Lady Booby as reputable gentlewoman and surreptitious siren, Mrs. Western as arch-strategist of politics and love, Square as paragon of humanist ethics, even Parson Adams as Christian Stoic: these are all "false vizors and habits" in which the character has invested something—in the more extreme cases, every-thing—of his sense of identity. Square's deathbed confession looks suspiciously like those convenient fifth-act conversions so familiar in eighteenth-century theater, but it has one important element of psychological probability: when the pressure of imminent death collapses Square's empty role as moral philoso-pher, he has no identity left, and so a complete turning of the soul is at least understandable.

In viewing character so frequently under the aspect of role playing, Fielding is both similar to and different from the predominant tradition of the novel. One reasonable way to talk about the distinctiveness of the novel's treatment of personality is to say that, from *Don Quixote* on, novels tend to be about people trying to play roles. That much-invoked modern formula, "crisis of identity," becomes at some point inevitable in discussing the novel generically because the novel was in fact born out of such a crisis. Cervantes' down-at-the-heels Spanish gentleman, living in the country with an old servant and a niece, tries to create for himself a role from literature because, as a rusting, functionless appurtenance of an iron age, he is no one in particular, and he wants desperately to become someone. The same is true, in different times and places, of a whole line of heroes of novels—Julien Sorel, Rastignac, Emma Bovary, Dorothea Brooke, Raskolnikov, Kafka's K., Leopold Bloom—all, whether pathetically or boldly, in search of an identity through the playing of a role. Even so prosaic a writer as Anthony Trollope offers us, in *The Last Chronicle of Barset*, a comprehensive vision of contemporary life in which one character after another, without either meaningful work or a firm sense of identity, tries to convince himself of his own existence by acting out some hackneyed part culled from literature. And among recent American novelists, writers as different as Saul Bellow, John Barth, Bernard Malamud, Walker Percy, have created protagonists who, unsure of who they are or what they can possibly become, try on roles like clothing.

In Fielding, however, the nearly ubiquitous role playing does not imply all that it does in other novelists. The one fundamental respect in which Fielding belongs to the neoclassical era and not to the unfolding age of the novel is in his ultimately assured sense of an ordered reality and of men's place in it. There is patently no "crisis" in Fielding's world, whether of identity or culture or anything else. The historic moment—for all the ingenious use of the rebellion of 1745 in *Tom Jones*—remains basically external to the moral and psychological predicament of the characters. The knavery and hypocrisy and gullibility of mankind are what they have always been—in the days of Lucian, in the days of Rabelais, in the days of Molière—and so they are finally knowable, manageable. The sense of identity in the protagonists of the novels, "those very few only showing their own faces," is strong, and even in the satiric figures whose identities are engulfed by the roles they play, the disturbing aspects of their radical lack of identity are consistently excluded by the external view taken of the characters and by the sense which the narrator conveys that all's well with *his* world, however morally flawed many of its individual creatures may be.

Role playing is presented not as the expression of an existential dilemma but as a Molièresque masquerade of deceptions in which the face of nature, though hidden, is always there behind the mask to be revealed. Cervantes, I think, no longer knows what nature is: his ability to translate this profoundest of uncertainties into fiction is a measure of the undying greatness of his novel. Fielding, less our contemporary than Cervantes in this important respect, is still confident in nature and what he knows of it; he goes on, in fact, in the sentence following the one already quoted from "The Characters of Men," to affirm this confidence—"For Nature, which unwillingly submits to the imposture, is ever endeavoring to peep forth and show herself." However inexhaustible the chicaneries of mankind, nature will out. It is on this premise that Fielding bases the firm unity of conception and presentation of both *Tom Jones* and *Joseph Andrews*, down to the revelation of true parentage and the matching of fit lovers— Nature peeping forth—at the end of each of the novels.

There is, then, in Fielding, a metaphysical certainty about identity which implies a novelistic certainty about character, so that character in his fiction is less fluctuating, finally less dynamic, than it is in the work of most other major novelists. This is, of course, a limitation upon his range in dealing with human problems, but, as in other things, he accomplishes a good deal more within his limits than we might at first expect. If most of his characters appear to exhibit flat, clear surfaces, his imagination and his method frequently enable him to see over to the other side of the surface showing. We have already observed something of this in his treatment of Black George and Jenny Jones; to explain this process more directly, I would like to begin by illustrating its operation on a rudimentary level in a relatively simple comic character, Mrs. Slipslop.

Slipslop, with her reddened skin, her udderlike breasts, her pimply face, swollen nose, and porcine eyes, with her pretensions to learning and her fierce determination to repay herself for all her years of cautious celibacy, is clearly a Hogarthian satiric figure, in both visual and moral terms. Though she plays a fairly minor role in the action of the novel, she positively bustles with life, principally, it would seem, because of the zest and joyful inventiveness with which Fielding has imagined her. But if one compares her to similar figures in Smollett, whose vitality could be explained in much the same way, a small but significant difference emerges. Mrs. Slipslop is egotistic, conniving, lustful, hypocritical, but there is some sense in the novel that even such a woman can be human. In contrast to Lady Booby, who is possessed by a kind of cold lust that seeks merely to use its objects for the gratification of body and ego, Mrs. Slipslop's lust could be called warm, for it does in one way connect her with humanity. Her malapropisms, which Fielding regularly italicizes, often unconsciously express a sort of tender contemplation of sensual pleasure, as when she terms Joseph "a strong healthy *luscious* boy" (I, 7), or when she comments on how innocent men, seduced by young wenches, "ever come to a *fragrant* punishment" (IV, 4). In her impassioned defense of Joseph's "fineness" to Lady Booby (IV, 6), the delight she takes in his physical attractiveness leads her to a real generosity that even enables her to transcend her habitual snobbishness. And her response to the story of Leonora and Horatio is a sensualist's altruism; with one lecherous eye on Joseph, who is sitting with her in the coach, she suggests that the only natural and decent thing for any woman to do with a handsome young fellow is to pity his plight and gratify his desire: "The woman must have no *compulsion* in her; I believe she is more of a Turk than a Christian; I am certain, if she had any Christian woman's blood in her veins, the sight of such a young fellow must have warmed it" (II, 5).

Slipslop's words take on particular ironic significance against the background of the whole novel, where there is a good deal of talk about Christians and Turks and what constitutes a true Christian, where that bony arm of the church militant, Parson Adams, is often made to wonder whether there are any real Christians left in England which, as it appears in the novel, could well be called the land of "the Christian specious," to borrow one of Slipslop's happiest slips (IV, 6). Fielding's notion of what makes a Christian is clearly not identical with Mrs. Slipslop's, but the two have something in common. Slipslop's *compulsion* does generate in her at least a limited kind of compassion, the word for which she comically mistakes it, and this is a greater degree of human openness than many of the self-proclaimed Christians in the book actually possess.

Fielding's ability to envisage both positive and negative aspects in his ostensibly one-sided characters is especially important in his presentation of the figures he wants us to admire. It is notoriously difficult for novelists to write convincingly about good people, but I think Fielding succeeds more than most readers have allowed with the models of good men in both his comic novels, Parson Adams and Squire Allworthy. Now, these two good men have generally impressed readers as virtual opposites: Adams is seen as that rare literary bird, an engaging True Christian Hero, boisterous and touchingly quaint in his essential nobility, while Squire Allworthy is usually found to be an unmitigated bore. Both these responses are, I think, accurate enough as far as they go, but misleadingly incomplete. For all the obvious differences between the two characterizations, they exhibit under close scrutiny an underlying similarity of conception and novelistic strategy.

A major emphasis in Fielding scholarship over the past two decades, partly in reaction to the long-standing image of a bawdy, rakish Fielding, has been upon the serious Christian tendency of his writing. The Christianizing critics have understandably seized on Abraham Adams as hero and the whole role of the clergy in *Joseph Andrews* as pearls of passing value. Martin Battestin has, it seems to me, conclusively shown that Fielding borrowed something from the recurrent biblical symbolism of Latitudinarian sermons for the general scheme of this novel: Father Abraham, the type of Christian charity, takes on the task of guiding Joseph, the type of Christian continence, on a kind of pilgrimage through a land of the Christian specious.[6] It is easy, however, to become too solemn about the Christian Fielding, and I am not altogether sure whether the feel for life and the moral imagination of his novels are in every regard so scrupulously Christian as it is now often assumed he meant them to be. In any case, Parson Adams, whose family name suggests an Edenic kind of patriarch, is astonishingly unseeing for a faithful guide and can be considered the moral hero of the novel only in a drastically qualified sense.

The clergyman possesses, as Fielding tells us in the Preface, "a character of perfect simplicity," that is, of complete innocence, and he is clearly endowed with a whole set of attributes Fielding would want all Christians to aspire to—unstinting generosity and compassion, benevolence, courage, firm faith and deep learning, adherence to a sane Anglicanism that eschews the high road to Romish heresy and the low road of the evangelical sects. At the beginning of I, 3, Fielding reiterates the essential "simplicity" of Adams' character; there, however, we already learn that this implies not just the opposite of duplicity but ignorance of the ways of men—hardly an ideal quality for a teacher and guide. What Fielding suggests through the character of Adams, as he does in a related way with Squire Allworthy, is that one must pay a price for being so perfectly good, or rather, that to be so good is not so good as it might appear.

Though Adams has the affection of his parishioners, he is in many ways painfully alienated from the world they inhabit. A man of books, and only books divine and classical, he repeatedly prefers the authority of the printed word to that of lived experience. For him, "later ages" means the time of Caesar; modern times, "these last thousand years" (II, 9). Even in his own home, he is out of touch with what is going on: when he tries to buttress his shaky authority as husband by quoting the Bible to his wife in order to remind her of her duties of submission, she roundly rebukes him, "It was blasphemy to quote Scripture out of church" (IV, 11). In a world of masks, subterfuge, false identities, he insists on taking appearance for reality. In a moral existence where so much must be apprehended through the doubleness of irony and paradox, his "simplicity" makes him incapable of grasping anything that looks like contradiction. The moment when, having interrupted his son's reading, he agrees, though baffled by the paradox, to place faith in the *ipse dixit* of the printed word, is paradigmatic of his whole relationship to reality: " 'But, good as this lady was, she was still a woman; that is to say, an angel, and not an angel.'—'You must mistake, child,' cries the parson, 'for you read nonsense.' 'It is so in the book,' answered the son. Mr. Adams was then silenced by authority, and Dick proceeded" (IV, 10).

Fielding discreetly implies, moreover, that to remain so perfectly innocent—and therefore so imperceptive—Parson Adams, for all his honest altruism, must be peculiarly focused on himself. He is interrupted, in an often cited episode, while preaching impromptu on Abraham's noble readiness to sacrifice his son, by the news of his own son's supposed drowning, and this throws him into a wild fit of despair (IV, 8). The effect of this sudden reversal is to elicit sympathy as well as amusement or satiric censure by showing us the gap between spiritual profession and human practice, stern ideal and compassionate actuality. But the whole passage ought to be compared with an earlier one—here again Fielding must be read backward as well as forward—in which Adams and Joseph are tied back to back, unable to extricate themselves, while Fanny is being hurried to the malicious squire's house by his henchmen to submit to his sexual pleasure (III, 11). Joseph of course is in agony, and Parson Adams tries to bring him to a sense of his duty to accept with equanimity the just decrees of Providence. " 'O sir!' cried Joseph, 'all this is very true, and very fine, and I could hear you all day, if I was not so grieved at heart as now I am.' 'Would you take physic,' says Adams, 'when you are well, and refuse it when you are sick?' " Especially in the light of Adams' subsequent failure to take physic himself in the needed hour, the high homiletic tone he adopts here toward Joseph, for all the piety and even benevolence of its motives, looks peculiarly unfeeling: it is a rare moment when Adams is less than attractive, his pious principle cutting him off from empathy with his young friend.

In this connection, it should be noted that, throughout, Fielding's "ideal Christian," though genuinely selfless in some ways, is egotistically fixed on his own learning, his own sermons, his own theories about life: "Indeed, if this good man had an enthusiasm, or what the vulgar call a blind side, it was this: he thought a schoolmaster the greatest character in the world, and himself the greatest of all schoolmasters, neither of which points he would have given up to Alexander the Great at the head of his army" (III, 5). Out of context, this might sound like megalomania; in context it simply means that the good parson is a charming whimsical egotist, but an inflexible egotist nevertheless. And we have seen, besides, that this is by no means the only respect in which Joseph's mentor may be said to have "a blind side." Parson Adams, in sum, can still be fairly described as one of the few completely engaging representations in fiction of a good Christian, a character of perfect simplicity, but much of his moral and psychological credibility derives from Fielding's artistic awareness that even perfect simplicity has its necessary complications, its ambiguities.

A similar awareness enriches his presentation of Squire Allworthy, though its application in the squire's case has the opposite effect of making the character less than engaging. A good many readers, I suspect, have been misled by the convention of quasi-allegorical names adopted by Fielding from English stage comedy into thinking that his characters were as simple as the neatly symbolic labels attached to them. Tom's foster father is, of course, intended to be an exemplary man, the charitable, conscientious Christian who is indeed allworthy, and the fact that he is avowedly modeled after Fielding's two esteemed friends and patrons suggests that he can hardly be meant as a satirical figure. But I think it is a demonstrable part of Fielding's design in the creation of Allworthy to show that in his case, too, a price is paid for goodness, a price, moreover, which at least at some moments must seem exorbitant in the warm and vivid world of *Tom Jones.*

When Allworthy speaks, he is repeatedly didactic. The eighteenth-century reader may possibly have had a higher tolerance for such edifying stuff than most of us possess today; yet Fielding is careful both to support and undercut his tireless moralizer, making apparent his own awareness that a solemn insistence on the truth, however sound, may be something of a bore. Thus, when Allworthy delivers his sermon—Fielding himself uses the word—to Dr. Blifil on tender friendship with a concern for worldly prudence as the proper basis for marriage (I, 12), he offers a serious thematic prelude to the major action of the novel, but Fielding sets off his message with an ambiguous suspicion of irony. Dr. Blifil, we are told, has been exerting the greatest effort to keep from laughing, and the whole sermon chapter concludes with this description of his response to Allworthy's words: "He now praised every period of what he had heard with the warmth of a young divine who hath the honour to dine with a bishop the same day in which his lordship hath mounted the pulpit." The satiric thrust of the statement is obviously directed at Dr. Blifil, an arrant schemer completely deaf to the ringing truths of reasonable virtue which Allworthy has just enunciated. But this does not altogether dispel the image of the squire mounting the pulpit in his own sitting room; there is something stiff, uncomfortably episcopal, about this good man, and Fielding is finely aware of it.

A bishop in the glory of his pulpit is hardly in the best position to see what is going on below stairs between Joan the chambermaid and Robin the hostler, and surely the greatest price Allworthy pays for his goodness is that he is, no less than Parson Adams, out of touch with the world immediately around him. His obtuseness, in failing to perceive the most palpable rascality in his own household for nearly twenty years, has often been commented on, but it should be fully recognized that this obtuseness has been purposefully contrived by the writer. When Mrs. Miller, in the final scene of discovery (VII, 2), cries out to Allworthy, "You are deceived, sir," her words reverberate against the entire novel. Allworthy has not only been imperceptive; in a few important instances he has also been presumptuous—as though Fielding wanted to suggest that one who lives out the ideal of the righteous life may on occasion run the risk of being righteous overmuch. One of the squire's principal responsibilities, after all, and one of the main causal elements in the plot, is the role he plays as justice of the peace, but twice we are explicitly informed that he has been acting in contradiction to the law, in excess of his authority. When Allworthy condemns and punishes Partridge for adultery (II, 6), Fielding takes pains to remind us, under the cover of a facetious aside, that the law does not admit the evidence of a wife for or against her husband, and, then, three paragraphs later, he tells us that Allworthy firmly accepts Partridge's guilt, which, for this magistrate, "the declaration of his wife that she had caught her husband in the fact, did sufficiently prove." Further on, when Allworthy condemns Molly Seagrim to Bridewell for fornication—in a moment Tom will obtain a remission of the sentence—the narrator makes it even clearer that Allworthy is disregarding the fixed legal limits of his own jurisdiction: "A lawyer may perhaps think Mr. Allworthy exceeded his authority a little in this instance. And, to say the truth, I question, as here was no regular information before him, whether his conduct was strictly regular. However, as his intention was truly upright, he ought to be excused in *foro conscientiae;* since so many arbitrary acts are daily committed by magistrates who have not this excuse to plead for themselves" (IV, 11).

It is worth noting how Fielding quietly extends the condition of being judged here from the accused to the magistrate himself: we are asked to excuse Allworthy in *foro conscientiae* precisely as we are asked to do with Tom, though perhaps Tom's transgressions may seem less objectionable because they are the result of what might be called an excess of compassion, while Allworthy's mistake stems from an excess of righteous zeal. In any case, it must be remembered that the errors for which Allworthy is pardoned before the bar of conscience have grave enough consequences to threaten irrevocable damage to the lives of five persons—Partridge, Jenny Jones, Molly, Tom, and Sophia, not to mention the formidable Mrs. Partridge, who suffers incidentally from her husband's punishment and then is conveniently killed off.

It is a revealing fact that Allworthy's mistaken judgments are connected with sexual activities deemed criminal, for there is nothing in the world of *Tom Jones* that he is more crucially out of touch with than its abundant and exuberant sexuality. The very first of his sermons is his discourse to Jenny on the evils of carnal indulgence (I, 7), introduced with an appropriately qualifying chapter heading, "Containing Such Grave Matter that the Reader Cannot Laugh Once through the Whole Chapter, Unless Peradventure He Should Laugh at the Author." This is not to suggest that Allworthy's defense of chastity is meant to be dismissed: the course of the novel in fact demonstrates that one invites trouble, as the squire warns Jenny, in allowing reason to be overpowered by sexual appetite. But there is something wrong with the tone of this moral lecture. When Allworthy dismisses the act of love as "a short, trivial, contemptible pleasure," Fielding would obviously subscribe to the first and probably even to the second epithet, at least in an attempt to place sex in perspective within his large system of values, but the author of *Tom Jones*, however Christian we make him, would surely not assent very readily to the contemptibility of a pleasure in which he could imagine such shared delight, such healthy naturalness, even when taken promiscuously. Or to put it another way, though Fielding might actually agree that a true Christian, thinking of the spiritual pleasures which are his greatest fulfillment, would hold the merely carnal ones in contempt, the moralizing attitude of "contemptible" in context, the deficiency of sympathetic imagination reflected in Allworthy's use of the word, are the stale distillations of preacher's ink, devoid of the juices of human experience.

At this point, in order to grasp the full meaning of Allworthy's personal limitations in the scheme of the novel, we must try to see him in relation to most of the other major characters. For one of Fielding's important technical innovations in *Tom Jones* was to systematize the procedure of comparing and contrasting characters which he had already used in *Joseph Andrews* and to make its significance felt virtually everywhere in the novel. The characters of *Tom Jones* are arranged in a more or less symmetrical, coherent system that extends over a complicated set of coordinates of meaning.

Within this system, the "flatness" of the various characters is completely functional and, in some cases, even begins to assume contours of roundness to the synoptic eye.

I am going to risk sounding gratuitously abstract for a moment by translating the central ethical theme of prudence in *Tom Jones* into the terms of what might be thought of as a sort of moral biology; since Fielding's elaborately unified scheme invites us to take large views, I trust the abstraction will justify itself. In *Tom Jones,* I would like to suggest, humanity is imagined under the aspect of energy; people are individuated largely in terms of their levels of energy and the ways they use or abuse that energy. By "energy" I mean something close to the old notion of "animal spirits" which was cherished by the theoretical physiology still current in Fielding's day. It is the vitality—physical, emotional, mental—that galvanizes an inert body into human liveliness; it is strongly appetitive, but not exclusively so; one of its most revealing and powerful expressions is in sexuality, but its meaning is not exhausted by sex. One might call it libido, in the proper Freudian sense, not in its popular simplification, but that would introduce certain assumptions alien to Fielding's whole understanding of human nature. In some mythical state of nature, this life energy would enjoy uninhibited expression, but in the restricting moral world we actually inhabit, complete spontaneity is not possible, and energy as Fielding imagines it must be coupled with restraint, which, in its positive aspect is moral prudence, in its chief negative aspect, calculating artifice. The major characters of *Tom Jones,* taken together, form a scheme of the possibilities of interplay between energy and restraint.

The two squires and the two lovers constitute a vertical group in the thematic center of the novel. At the top is Squire Allworthy, who is all civilized restraint, the embodiment of the moral man, but who lacks—and fails to understand—the energy that informs the world below him. (He is, we remember, not only impeccably celibate in his long years as a widower but also childless, for all the troupe of bastards Western fantastically attributed to him: his virtue is admirable but there is something sterile about the man.) At the bottom is Squire Western, who is all unrestrained energy, impetuous and often wildly misdirected: he is the Atlas of the novel on whose broad and presumably hairy back everything else rests. Tom Jones's place on this vertical scale of energy and restraint would be above Squire Western: he has something of that quality of control which makes his uncle the novel's complete civilized man, but it is often swept aside by the powerful impetus of his passions and appetites. Above Tom and below Squire Allworthy on the vertical scale is Sophia, whose abundant energy is evidenced by her healthy desire for Tom, by her capacity for bold action and spontaneous feeling, but who generally keeps natural impulse under the firm control of civilized restraint.[7]

Other, subsidiary, groupings of characters, who are viewed in a sharper satirical perspective, suggest themselves. Because these secondary characters are more consistently subjected to moral exposure, it is understandable that the meaning of "energy" in their case tends to be more strictly limited to sexuality. The women of the novel display a variety of combinations of female artifice and sexual impulse. At the top of this group is Aunt Western, in whom sexuality has been absorbed by female artifice, or as we say, sublimated, so that even the relationship between the sexes is seen by this politician as a matter of military strategy. Below her, in descending degree of artifice and ascending degree of raw sexual energy, are: Lady Bellaston, whose sexual appetite itself seems a kind of artificiality, consciously stimulated and sustained beyond its time; Bridget Allworthy, who artfully conceals the strongly carnal aspect of her character; Mrs. Waters, who, despite a modicum of female artifice, is a woman of healthy energy not only in her sexual desires but also in the uncalculating impulses

of the Good Heart she possesses; Molly Seagrim, who combines
a simple animal urge for sexual satisfaction with merely the
crudest kind of female artifice and pretense. The two tutors of
the Allworthy household and their prize pupil form still another group: Blifil, whose flow of energy is a thin, mean
trickle, and whose sexuality is diverted into sadistic fantasies
and onanistic gratifications; Square, who hypocritically conceals his very real lust; Thwackum, who, "not only strictly
chaste in his own person, but a great enemy to the opposite
vice in all others" (V, 10), channels his vigorous energy into
the hard-clenched violence of a schoolmaster's sadism.

Against this whole scheme, it should be more apparent than
it has been why Squire Western is so important in energizing
the whole novel, literally and figuratively. He is, to shift the
mythical comparison, the Silenus of *Tom Jones*, the perambu-
lating reservoir of that uncivilized, pre-moral energy which
works through the other characters in varying systems of restraint, blockage, distribution, and camouflage. With a perfect
integrity of imagination, Fielding is able to adapt even the
most obvious comic stage devices to this underlying conception of the character. Thus, Squire Western's actions and
gestures abound in the sort of mechanical repetitions that
Bergson observed in Molière and saw as the essence of the
ridiculous. "D——n me if shatunt, d——n me if shatunt," Western says again and again in sheer inarticulate fury over Sophia's
refusal to marry Blifil, and he is scarcely more articulate in
repeatedly using his hunter's ear-splitting hollo indiscriminately
on foxes and human beings. But such repetitions, far from
reducing him to a mechanical puppet, make him seem more
fully what he is: a center of continually detonating energy
that can scarcely be contained in anything so conscious, so
premeditated, as human language. Western's vocabulary consists of full-throated cries, half-growled snatches of dialect,
hearty blows or handshakes, allusions to, and demonstrations
of, the less polite functions of the body. He refutes an argu-

ment of his sister's in a manner that is wholly characteristic:
"'Ho! are you come back to your politics? . . . as for those
I despise them as much as I do a f____t.' Which last words he
accompanied and graced with the very action, which, of all
others, was the most proper to it" (VII, 3). Western as the
embodiment of earthy energy, we can see from this instance,
is aptly translated into an imagery of explosion. He is, I am
tempted to say, energy represented as the simple physiological
reflex of male explosion, but the recurrent image of a popping
squire is not strictly sexual, only analogous to the sudden
release of virile energy in sex, as when Western begins to
speak after impatiently hearing out Allworthy, "the froth burst-
ing forth from his lips the moment they were uncorked" (XVII,
3).

As an explosive figure of energy, Western is both thoroughly
engaging and a wonderfully absurd object lesson in the necessity to direct and channel human energy rationally. He is
forever at dizzying cross-purposes with himself, setting out
for Sophia and ending up with the foxes, sincerely protesting
his supreme concern for his daughter's happiness in one breath
and swearing he will whip her naked into the streets in the
next.

The fact that Squire Western is this bundle of raw impulses gives him a double role in the plot of the novel. On
the one hand, he is obviously the classic comic *senex*, the
father who insists on marrying off his daughter for money
and who therefore is the roadblock in the way of the natural
union that is the comedy's destined end. But for all the violence of his temporary opposition to the lovers, his primary
role is master of the revels in the novel, as he is master of
the hunt. At the beginning of the book and again at the
end, we hear him urging on the pursuit of "puss," which is
hunter's slang for the fox, and, then as now, the term used
by a rather different kind of huntsman for the female sexual
part. Western himself insists on the connection between the

two varieties of chases in his vocal encouragement of both. After the pitched battle in the woods with Thwackum and Blifil, he heartily approves of Tom as a "liquorish dog," beats the bushes for the wench, crying, "Soho! Puss is not far off," invites all the combatants to make peace over a bottle, and responds to a suggestion of Thwackum's that the country should be cleared of such "vermin" as Molly by extending the comparison: "I would as soon rid the country of foxes . . . I think we ought to encourage the recruiting those numbers which we are every day losing in the war" (V, 12). It is entirely appropriate that Western should blithely attribute bastards to his acquaintances, including even the morally and physically neuter Parson Supple, that he should repeatedly refer to his own daughter as "meat" and to the conjugal "tousling" he thinks she is squeamish about, and, finally, that at the end of the novel he should be sitting downstairs merrily swilling his liquor, during and long after "that happy hour which . . . surrendered the charming Sophia to the eager arms of her enraptured Jones" (XVIII, 13).

In the prefatory chapter to Book V, Fielding speaks of a "vein . . . of contrast, which runs through all the works of creation" and which plays an important role in making both natural and artificial beauty apparent to us: "for what demonstrates the beauty or excellence of anything but its reverse?" As usual, Fielding goes on to qualify the seriousness of his aesthetic generalization with a display of facetiousness, but he has in fact offered us one of the keys to his novelistic method. The vein of contrast is worked through his fiction in many ways, some of which we had occasion to observe in considering his style. In the deployment of characters, one of its most important expressions is in the very nature of Squire Western, who acts as a rapidly moving, exploding principle of contrast in scene after scene. His first encounter with Lord Fellamar vividly illustrates the juxtaposition of comic opposites that we see also in his confrontations with his sister, with Parson Supple, with Allworthy:

"Sir, I am Lord Fellamar," answered he, "and am the happy man whom I hope you have done the honour of accepting for a son-in-law."

"You are a son of a b____," replied the squire, "for all your laced coat. You my son-in-law, and be d____n'd to you!"

"I shall take more from you, sir, than from any man," answered the lord; "but I must inform you that I am not used to hear such language without resentment."

"Resent my a____," quoth the squire. "Don't think I am afraid of such a fellow as thee art! because has got a spit there dangling at thy side. Lay by your spit, and I'll give thee enough of meddling with what doth not belong to thee. I'll teach you to father-in-law me. I'll lick thy jacket." (XV, 5).

Western's incorrigible crudeness, his booby squire's ignorance of the simplest decencies of polite intercourse, are transparently and delightfully revealed, but the rich humor of Fielding's contrasts works both ways, and by juxtaposition with the squire's rawness, the mincing, artificial quality of Lord Fellamar's recitation of social formulas becomes apparent. Squire Western in London is like a blast of fresh air, at its most effective setting askew masks and baring the plain features behind polite pretense. One moment in a mocking description by Western of Lady Bellaston's circle is a perfect paradigm of his positive satiric function in the novel. He expresses his unmitigated scorn for the whole "kennel of hoop-petticoat b____s," and, angrily mimicking the polite ladies, he refers to Lady Bellaston, in quoting her, as "that fat a____se b____" (XVII, 3). The novel nowhere offers a physical description of Lady Bellaston: we have seen her in action as the flirtatious masquerader (another figure for whom mask is identity), the proud intriguer, the jealous hostess, the elegant and munificent sensualist well past her prime, but here she is suddenly brought down hard to earth—Squire Western is never anywhere else—as "that fat a____se b____," and the coarse physical characterization adds a new perspective to our vision of her.

The same principle of contrast operates in connecting the

man at the top of the novel, Squire Allworthy, with the man at the bottom of the novel, Squire Western, and that is why it is important to see how Western fits into the whole scheme of characters in order to complete an assessment of Allworthy. Fielding delights in setting these two opposites side by side, but he intends a dialectic relationship between them, not just a satiric exposure of Squire Western. If Western seems unreasonable, ignorant, crude, greedy, even a little crazy, alongside Allworthy, the more exemplary squire has a look of starched formality, an excessive correctness, in comparison with his enthusiastic neighbor. "Madam," Allworthy addresses Sophia before her wedding in a sort of official benediction, "I am convinced you have bestowed yourself on one who will be sensible of your great merit, and who will at least use his best endeavours to deserve it." To which Western loudly rejoins, "His best endeavours! . . . that he will, I warrant un. Harkee, Allworthy, I'll bet thee five pounds to a crown we have a boy to-morrow nine months" (XVII, 12). Allworthy's compliment to Sophia is elegant, tactful, and properly moral, but Western's rough evocation of marriage bed and fruitful union seems much more in the spirit of the comic consummation of the novel.

The relationship of contrast and mutual qualification between the novel's two squires suggests that antithesis and balance are the basic principle of characterization as of style in *Tom Jones*. We have viewed some of the chief characters vertically as they relate to the category of energy; it is also possible to view them horizontally, in terms of the pairings and contrasts of characters and groups of characters. In this respect, the novel is organized around the two Somerset households, both ruled over by prosperous widowers. Each household has its attendant clergyman—the wrathful Thwackum and the obsequious Supple. In each household there are tutors for the young—Square and Thwackum, an antithesis within an antithesis, over against Aunt Western (who is also part of another pairing in her role as formidable virgin sister opposite Bridget, an imposing sister in her own, not exactly virginal, fashion). The tutors, in turn, have pairs of pupils, each composed of a "good" pupil and a "bad" one—Blifil, who is the perfect disciple of his hypocritical pedagogues, and Tom, who manfully resists their spuriously moral education, over against Mrs. Fitzpatrick, who takes to her aunt's tenets of worldliness, and Sophia, who manages to ignore them.

The methods of instruction, with their differing effects on different pupils, raise the question of nature and nurture as influences in the formation of character. Blifil and Tom have the same mother, but both seem to take after their fathers, Blifil's having been a scheming rascal and Tom's a decent, if somewhat incontinent, young man.[8] Heredity in this way prepares one child to thrive under a tutelage in hypocrisy, the other to reject it. Sophia combines two very different hereditary strains—her father's crude energy is chastened and refined by the gentility and accommodating disposition she inherits from her mother, so that she has a healthily balanced temperament impervious to her aunt's influence. About Mrs. Fitzpatrick's parents we are told nothing, though the fact that they are nowhere in evidence while she lives with her aunt would seem to indicate that she was orphaned at an early age and so more easily influenced by a self-appointed tutor. In any case, she is flighty by nature (her childhood nickname was "Miss Giddy"), so with her, as with Blifil, heredity and environment would appear to work together to produce a morally unreliable character. Because the intractable pupil in each of the pairs serves as a kind of "control," one can infer that for each of the young people nature, not nurture, is ultimately decisive. This, of course, should hardly surprise us in a writer whose social imagination is essentially conservative, as is Fielding's.

The general procedure of pairing characters is one of the important ways in which *Tom Jones* constitutes an imaginative assimilation and transformation of the achievement of *Don Quixote*. Cervantes' novel would have been Fielding's first model for the shaping of fiction around a richly active antithesis, a dialectic, of character, but Fielding, with a love of symmetries and a feeling for coherent systems unlike anything in Cervantes, translated the method of *Don Quixote* into an intricately balanced scheme. A symptom of the nature of this transformation is the fact that within the neat structure of parallel households which we have been considering, there are *two* Sancho-Quixote pairs. The obvious one is the heroic and romantic Tom and the fearful and superstitious Partridge who, despite his pseudo learning, has an earthy side as well: "Who knows, Partridge," rhapsodizes Tom, "but the loveliest creature in the universe may have her eyes now fixed on that very moon which I behold this instant?" "Very likely, sir . . . and if my eyes were fixed on a good sirloin of roast beef, the devil might take the moon and her horns into the bargain" (VIII, 9). Symmetrically parallel to this male Sancho-Quixote combination is a female pair of the same nature, in which Honour plays exactly the role vis à vis Sophia that Partridge does for Tom: " 'Would not you, Honour, fire a pistol at any one who should attack your virtue?' 'To be sure Ma'am . . . one's virtue is a dear thing, especially to us poor servants; for it is our livelihood, as a body may say; yet I mortally hate fire-arms' " (VII, 7).

It is clear that such exchanges are, to borrow Fielding's own phrase from the title page of *Joseph Andrews*, "written in imitation of the manner of Cervantes," but there is an underlying neatness of conception and execution not at all characteristic of Cervantes. The neatness makes itself felt in the smallest details, where the vein of contrast sometimes runs with geometrical regularity, as in the comparison of Sophia's hands, "which had every property of snow in them, except that of melting," with Honour's, which show "an exact resemblance, in cold and colour, to a piece of frozen beef" (X, 3). The neatness is also manifest in the broad symmetry with which the various pairings of the Allworthy and Western families are set against each other.

What has to be considered, in order to get a better sense of Fielding's place as a novelist, is how this symmetry is functional in his novel. Part of the reason it is there at all, I suppose, is because of that fundamental aesthetic preference for balanced antithesis which we observed in connection with Fielding's style, but that is not exactly a novelistic justification for the meticulous symmetries. The parallels and contrasts do heighten our awareness, as I have tried to indicate briefly, of the novel's moral themes and the way individual characters reflect them. In fact, the whole procedure of deploying characters in matched opposites could be taken as a translation into narrative structure of Aristotelian ethics, a kind of spatial illustration of the need for golden means, but wisdom suggests that this interpretation should not be pressed too hard. The most general function of the careful symmetries, it seems to me, is to show forth the relatedness of all the characters to each other and to the moral and social concerns of the novel. Now, many novelists have sought to interrelate all their characters, even those who do not come in direct contact with each other, but for Fielding the relatedness must seem tight, necessary, fully coherent, and to make it so he needs the kind of neatness we have been observing. Implicit in the very desire to relate personages in this way is, once more, a sense of certainty about the intelligibility of mankind which we may no longer share, but this reflection of Fielding's neoclassical assumptions surely need not imply any doubt about his artistic integrity. On the contrary, one of the chief means he uses to make manifest in art his magisterial knowledge of his characters and the passions that move them is just this neatly symmetrical plan. What is most important to note here, however, in regard to Fielding's role in the development of the genre, is that he is the first novelist anywhere to conceive the novel in genuinely architectonic terms. In order to see how consistently and inventively he carries out this conception in his two comic novels, we ought to go on now to consider his handling of plot, theme, and strategies of narration.

A novel is another kind of work.
Unity of design is its character . . .
A combination of incidents, entertaining in
themselves, are made to form a whole; and an
unnecessary circumstance becomes a blemish,
by detaching from the simplicity which is
requisite to exhibit the whole to advantage.
—*Thomas Holcroft, Preface to* Alwyn, or the Gentleman Comedian

4. THE ARCHITECTONIC NOVEL

Both the greatness and the weakness of the novel as a genre are intimately connected with its voracious, indiscriminate appetite for reality. The supreme achievements of the genre command our imagination through their titanic capaciousness; over against the expansive genius of *Don Quixote*, *Moby-Dick*, *The Brothers Karamazov*, *War and Peace*, *The Magic Mountain*, *Remembrance of Things Past*, those slender, perfectly wrought novels like Ford Madox Ford's *The Good Soldier* or Gide's *Pastoral Symphony* appear almost to avoid the real challenge of the genre, seem finally a little precious. But one hardly wants to blame novelists for tightly circumscribing their own scope, since in many cases they are impelled by a keen awareness of the treacherous quicksand that the novel's bigness can become for a writer. If the big novel has led to a unique kind of literary greatness, it has more often encouraged a sort of literary gigantism—excessive growth accompanied by muscular weakness and impotence—which has affected even some very gifted writers, from Richardson and Rousseau to

Balzac, to Faulkner at his turgid worst and Thomas Wolfe except at his best. For if the novelist's impulse to include is repeatedly allowed to dominate his sense of responsibility to select, he is often likely to give us a welter of details, a tide of rhetoric, from which no artistically coherent pattern emerges.

This danger is compounded by the "formal realism" which, according to a prevalent critical view, is one of the distinguishing characteristics of the genre. That somewhat confusing term refers to the way novelists tend to adopt for their own fictional form some simulation of a "form" of real life, whether in the documentary record of a set of events or in the kaleidoscopic movements of the mind itself. But formal realism, when literally taken over into fiction, might more properly be called realistic formlessness, for the data of reality have no intrinsic structure of the kind that, ever since Aristotle, has been assumed to be the first prerequisite for a work of art. *Moll Flanders* and *Roxana* are brilliant acts of journalistic ventriloquism, extended impersonations of real people, but in using the mere sequence of events of one person's life as their unifying form, they lack the imaginative integrity, the revelatory power, of the most serious literary art. At the other end of the history of the novel, a good deal of avant-garde fiction since Beckett suffers from an analogous deficiency because its formal realism leads to a direct reproduction of the meaninglessness, the labyrinthine deviations and frustrations, of the writers' mental and moral worlds; even incoherence, it would seem, calls for a certain coherence of craft if it is to be expressed artistically. Most novelists of stature, to be sure, have found ways to give some artistic shape to the formal realism of their narratives, but an overriding commitment to reproducing the verbal texture, the structural fluidity, the repetitiousness, of reality, often dulls the writer's sense of selectivity, so that he cannot distinguish what is not artistically functional in his own style, in his own accumulation of episodes and details.

Formal realism, I would like to suggest, is not so dependable a measure of the novel at its distinctive best as criticism after James has tended to assume. How does it help us, after all, to explain the profound innovation of *Don Quixote?* This first of novels, which with the passage of time looms larger and larger as the archetype of all that follows, is avowedly the work of a book-writing narrator—in fact, a narrator presenting the material of still another narrator—and we are continually made aware of how the narrator imposes patterns on the stuff of reality, playing with the ambiguous status of his book as art-or-reality. Indeed, it could be argued that the real subject of the novel—and the key to its protean form—as the characteristic genre of a post-traditionalist age of skepticism, is the stubborn ambiguity of the relationship between literary creation and reality. If this does not apply equally well to all novels, it works about as often as any of the textbook generalizations on the novel: one could easily trace a Great Tradition, with very different emphases from Mr. Leavis', from Cervantes to Fielding to Sterne and Diderot, and on to Joyce and Nabokov.

Fielding, as we have already had occasion to observe, is continuously and finely conscious of the status of his novels as artifacts. He punctuates his writing with heightened reminders of this status—in the parodistic elements of his style, in the prefatory material and the chapter headings, in the more obtrusive manifestations of the self-dramatizing narrator, in the repeated allusions to traditional literary practice.

Now, novelists in general have often called their readers' attention to the contrast between literature, which is a mere representation of reality, and their own work, which the reader is encouraged to think of as life itself. It is hardly a coincidence that a number of important novelists—Cervantes, Fielding, Jane Austen, Thackeray—started out writing parodies, for the sense of realism in the novel often depends upon a parodist's awareness of the awkward disparity between things as they really are and things as they are conventionally represented in literature. Thus, in a characteristic parenthesis in *Tom Jones* (XII, 6), we are told that the moon had begun "to put forth her silver light, as the poets call it (though she looked at that time more like a piece of copper)," for Fielding, like other novelists, knowingly writes about a world where traditional silver and gold have been superseded by the baser metals which, if less resplendent than the fixed currency of conventional literature, are decidedly more varied and interesting.

The particular tradition of the novel, however, in which Fielding figures significantly, generally proceeds by pointing up a contrast not between life and its representation in literature but between one kind of representation of reality and another. (It is surely this aspect of Fielding, more than anything else, that explains Gide's avid interest in him.) Literary works may pretend that they are reality itself, but from Fielding's point of view, this is in a way a foolish pretense, for, with his Aristotelian background, he was very conscious that any fiction is inevitably a made thing, an imitation of a human action that has been given order and wholeness and structural solidity by the craft of the maker. In this central respect, the epic may have been a decisive influence on him, not as a model for specific procedures, but as a basis for his entire conception of the genre and its relation to reality.

What Fielding does, then, in shaping both his comic novels is continually to exploit the artfully fashioned condition of the literary thing he is making, not only in the manipulation of style, but in the structure of the narrative, the texture of the narration, the juxtaposition and repetition of narrated events, the deployment of thematic materials. The introduction into *Joseph Andrews* and *Tom Jones* of actual pieces of literature, whether by quotation or allusion, which parallel the action of the novel, is especially instructive in this connection. Though the strategy is not used often enough to be thought of as a working model for Fielding's general novelistic technique, as two recent critics tend to imply,[1] it does, I think, provide a kind of key to his assumptions about the medium. The ingenuity of the parallels, when they occur, is admirable, but their artistic function is not so easy to explain as might first appear. A patently artificial representation of an action similar to the one we have been following in the novel is likely to strengthen our belief in the "reality" which the writer has created, much the way the play within a play works in Shakespeare. But Fielding's use of this procedure generally moves us toward an awareness of the different possibilities of representing reality in art rather than toward a simple assent to the authority of an art more verisimilar than the conventional sort.

A case in point is one of Lady Bellaston's dramatic entrances onto the scene of the novel (XIII, 4), heralded by the thunderous pounding at the door of her footman. The narrator pretends to be at a loss for words to describe that terrific sound, and so he resorts to quotation—"*Non acuta/Sic geminant Corybantes aera.* The priests of Cybele do not so rattle their sounding brass." The scrap of Latin verse quoted and translated alludes, of course, to the orgiastic cult of the great mother goddess, Cybele. Fielding offers it to us as a literary joke with a satiric point: Lady Bellaston might easily be thought of as a comical mother goddess, with her penchant for "adopting" younger men to serve her needs. (The literary joke, moreover, could well have a double point. The poem in which this line and a half appears is the ode of Horace—*Carminum,* Liber I, XVI—that begins: "*O matre pulchra filia pulchrior*—O maiden, more beautiful than your beautiful mother.") Unlike the Cybele of the ancient world, whose celebrants castrated themselves as the highest act of devotion to her, this aging, broad-bottomed goddess prefers her worshipers potent, though, from another point of view, she has a kind of emasculating effect in keeping them financially dependent upon her.

The literary past is superimposed on the present here in a characteristically Augustan manner: the lofty past is used to comment satirically on the fallen present, while we are kept aware of the condition of both as literary creations. Cybele herself does not appear, only the Latin poet's attempt, and the novelist's after him, to describe a sound of fury. Lady Bellaston is not meant to seem "more real" than Cybele—just as, say, Joyce's Gertie McDowell is neither more nor less real than Homer's Nausicaa. The fleeting juxtaposition, however, of the lady and the goddess, or perhaps, of the lady and Horace's *filia,* is piquant, because we glimpse opposite ends of the range of female types susceptible of representation in literature and of the literary modes through which they may be represented.

A more elaborate instance of Fielding's use of literary parallel is the song sung by Joseph Andrews (II, 12) just before the first reunion of the lovers. Fanny is seated at the fire next to Parson Adams, who is absorbed in his Aeschylus, when she hears a voice singing from one of the inner rooms of the inn. The song itself, with its familiar plea by a woestruck Strephon to the sweet nymph Chloe, its thronging Graces, soft Zephyrs, and myriad Loves dancing in train, is conventional enough to tempt a reader to skim it, but he does so at his own loss. These are the last two stanzas:

> My soul, whilst I gaze, is on fire,
>   But her looks were so tender and kind:
> My hope almost reach'd my desire,
>   And left lame Despair far behind.
> Transported with madness I flew
>   And eagerly seiz'd on my bliss;
> Her bosom but half she withdrew,
>   But half she refus'd my fond kiss.
>
> Advances like these made me bold;
>   I whisper'd her, "Love,—we're alone";

The rest let immortals unfold:
    No language can tell but their own.
Ah, Chloe, expiring, I cried,
    How long I thy cruelty bore!
Ah, Strephon, she blushing replied,
    You ne'er was so pressing before.

The song belongs to that peculiar subgenre so fashionable after the Restoration, developed with particular felicity by Dryden—the sophisticated erotic poem in an ostensibly pastoral mode. The soul on fire inevitably rhymes with—indeed, is almost equated with—desire. "Bliss" tends to be limited to the technical sexual meaning which it has in Dryden's songs; the "expiring" that Strephon undergoes is a familiar elegant variation on "dying," that is, achieving orgasm; and there is at least the suspicion of a double entendre in the blushing Chloe's final words, "You ne'er was so pressing before." The action represented in the poem obviously recapitulates the action of the whole novel (and it is perhaps not accidental that it should be introduced shortly before the midpoint of the narrative): the lovers in the song, frustrated by separation, at last fly to each other's arms and consummate their love. In a moment, Joseph will enter the room and actually clasp Fanny in his arms, imitating, within permitted limits, the end of the song and prefiguring the unchecked fulfillment at the end of the novel.[2]

For all the ingenuity of the parallels, there is an odd disparity between the tone of the poem and the nature of the novel's two lovers. One can safely assume that the song is one Joseph learned while applying himself, as the narrator has noted earlier, to the study of music in London. It in fact combines the opposite spheres of town and country which constitute one of the central thematic contrasts of the novel. The allusions of the poem are all to the country, but this elegant pastoral, in its polished literary artifice, its sophisticated

explicitness-through-obliquity about sexual gratification, is a
worldly creation of the city, lacking the essential quality of
innocence of the young country lovers, Joseph and Fanny,
whose reunion it adumbrates. What Fielding offers us is a
kind of experiment in different modes of representing the
same action. The decorum of his narrative will not allow him
to show us Joseph "expiring" with Fanny at the end of the
novel, but we get a teasing glimpse of that here. More important, we see the operation, side by side, of two diametrically
opposed kinds of literary artifice—the self-conscious sophistication of the smooth verses in which Strephon pants his way
to his ambrosial Chloe, and the relaxed, congenial artifice,
with cunning echoes of the erotic-pastoral vocabulary, through
which the narrator familiarly addresses his reader as he describes the agitation and embrace of Joseph and Fanny.

And Parson Adams, we should not forget, is a third element
in this scene. While literature is speaking to life over his head
—for amorous matters generally go over his head—he is en-
grossed in another kind of literature, the high, austere, and
distant art of Aeschylus, which effectively abstracts him from
the scene. When Fanny topples over backward from her chair
at the sight of Joseph, Adams leaps up and flings his Aeschylus into the fire in confusion. It is tempting to read this as
a neatly symbolic if temporary act of renunciation, the grave
scholar casting away his book in a spontaneous impulse to
help his friend. I am not altogether sure whether this action,
which is contrived as a farcical counterpoint to the emotion
of the lovers' reunion and has no significant repercussions, will
bear such symbolic freight. In any case, it is clear that the
presence of Aeschylus serves to remind us of still other possibilities of literary expression and of relations between literature and experience. Aeschylus is patently irrelevant to this
particular experience: it insulates Adams from his surroundings,
so that he is set at comical cross-purposes with himself; fails,
as usual, to see what is going on in time; and even loses the

precious book itself, actuality, as it were, consuming a merely literary version of human experience.

Fielding's use of literary parallels, however, has a more general function, which is to extend the unity of design of the whole novel, to reinforce through similarity in variety our sense that the novel has, in fact, a coherent structure. Joseph's song is not the only occasion on which his relationship with Fanny is reflected, or rather, refracted, in verse. At the very moment when Fanny is being spirited away by the henchmen of the scheming squire, during the debate between the poet and the player which seems entirely an irrelevant interlude, the player chooses to recite the following lines of Nathaniel Lee:

—No more; for I disdain
All pomp when thou art by—far be the noise
Of kings and crowns from us, whose gentle souls
Our kinder fates have steered another way.
Free as the forest birds we'll pair together,
Without remembering who our fathers were. (III, 10).

And on he goes, about flying to arbors, grots, and flowery meads to enjoy soft hours of bliss. The verses offer an idyllic image of Fanny and Joseph's as yet unfulfilled longings: the novel's two lovers, who literally have forgotten who their fathers are, find themselves separated by the snares and trammels of society, and the general movement of the novel is from the city toward the country setting where they will at last unite. For the moment, however, as the player recites these hazily beautiful lines, the lovers seem fatally sundered, with Fanny on her way to be raped. There is, admittedly, no really illuminating revelation of character or theme effectuated by this unexpected parallel and ironic counterpoint, but they serve to assure us that even the details of an interlude are not wholly extraneous to the novel, that a unity of design is being sustained.

The interpolated stories in both *Joseph Andrews* and *Tom Jones* need to be seen in the same light as the introduction of such literary parallels. The notion of using interpolated tales was clearly suggested to Fielding by the practice of Cervantes, Lesage, Marivaux, and others of his predecessors, though the tradition he adopted from them created special problems in his own fiction. For in the picaresque novels, with their easy, almost improvised linkage of episodes, the interpolated tales fall into place naturally as fictional diversions, varying the mood and mode of the main narrative. Fielding, on the other hand, was faced with the difficulty of integrating the tales into the structure of a carefully planned novel without causing undue structural stress, and I think he succeeded only in part because the convention of interpolation was not entirely compatible with the scrupulous unity of design which was his own innovation as a novelist. In any case, it is worth considering what he tried to do to assimilate the interpolated tale into his kind of fiction.

Basically, the use of interpolation is another reflection of his awareness of the novel as a made thing. Any product of literary craft has textures, woven out of words by the craftsman, and Fielding has a decided aesthetic interest in contrasted narrative textures, which he takes pains to bring out by placing the interpolated tales in relief against the surrounding action. The language and the conventions of the interpolated stories are intended to recall certain vogues of literature—especially, the fashionable romance and the cautionary tale—very different from Fielding's own experiment in creating a comic prose epic. The style of the interpolated material tends to be both formal and formulaic, with none of the animated inventiveness of the novel's main narrator; even the exchanges between characters within the interpolations are recitations of formal periods, not novelistic dialogue; and, by contrast, the surrounding narrative is made to seem both livelier and more lifelike than it otherwise would. Fielding heightens this intrinsic contrast by repeatedly breaking into his interpolations, giving us, in other words, artfully interrupted interruption.

Thus, in *Joseph Andrews,* when the lady in the stagecoach recounts "The History of Leonora, or the Unfortunate Jilt," we get not only a conventional tale of romantic disappointment, but a whole gallery of comic responses to it, one plane of literature interacting with another. Parson Adams puzzles over the identity of "this squire Horatio" and later denounces the "more than Corinthian assurance" of Leonora; the snobbish "Miss Grace-airs" injects her own acid words on the "forward slut" who is the subject of the story; and Mrs. Slipslop thrusts her usual malapropisms into the elegant progress of the tale while bemoaning the unfulfilled lovers with the empathy of a woman who has been too long deprived of a man. These temporary interruptions of the interpolation are augmented by an extended one: the chapters which begin and conclude "The History of Leonora" are separated by a chapter devoted to explosive farce and racy social comedy (II, 5); right in the middle of the conventional romantic action and formally stylized language of Leonora's tale, we get a traditional picaresque episode, a wild-swinging free-for-all in a country inn, with violent oaths, torn hair and clothing, and a baptism in hog's blood for the good parson. Fielding's strategies for bringing out contrasts in narrative texture are most conspicuous here, but he applies the same principle in Parson Adams' innocent exclamations over Mr. Wilson's story and in Partridge's persistent and impertinent interruptions of the Man of the Hill.

Fielding is interested, moreover, in the possibilities of repeating the design of the whole novel in the interpolated tales, though he carries out this aim more consistently and meticulously in *Tom Jones* than in *Joseph Andrews.* The one interpolation in the earlier novel that has a clear thematic function is Mr. Wilson's story; it is used to focus the central town-and-country polarity of the novel through the career of Joseph's father, who, unlike the son, is corrupted by the town, but finally emerges from London's moral morass to retire happily to the country with his beloved wife, as Joseph also will do. The story of Leonora relates more obliquely to the main action in pointing up the dangers of seeking to marry out of vain and worldly motives; and the truncated tale of Paul and Leonard, read by little Dick toward the end of the book, can be connected to the plot of the novel only by the most determined overinterpretation.[3] In *Tom Jones*, on the other hand, the two long interpolated tales carefully reflect the main action of the novel: both Tom and Sophia, on their way to the dangerous sphere of city life, listen to monitory stories of young people seduced by worldliness, the Man of the Hill serving as a weaker Tom, embittered by experience, and Mrs. Fitzpatrick as a frailer Sophia. The narrative of the Man of the Hill provides an especially apt illustration of Fielding's firm sense of structure, and it is worth looking at more closely.

The parallels between the Man of the Hill's story and Tom's are more elaborately worked out than the similar parallels between Joseph and Mr. Wilson. The old man was given in his youth, like Tom, to amorous indulgence and carelessness about money, though this leads him to an actual crime, not merely an imputed offense to feeling, and he flees to the city, estranged, he imagines, from his father. In London, living with a mistress, he is reduced to a state of dire want, and he comments retrospectively, with Tom assenting emphatically, that it is a horrible curse to see a woman you love in distress, to realize you have brought her to that state, and to be unable to relieve her. City life utterly corrupts him— again, in pointed contrast to Tom, who is embarrassingly compromised, but not really corrupted, by the role of gigolo he plays for Lady Bellaston. At this point in his London career, the Man of the Hill rescues a stranger who has been attacked by thieves, and this person turns out to be his father. A reconciliation follows, he reforms and returns to the country. The crossroads encounter through which he saves his father's life and is reunited with him reverses the Oedipus story, where a son unwittingly kills his father in an accidental meeting,[4] and later Fielding will offer us a different averted parallel to Oedipus in the incest his foundling hero imagines he has committed with Mrs. Waters. The reunion in the city of father and son, who afterward return together to the country, of course also prefigures the reconciliation in London of Tom and Squire Allworthy. Finally, the Man of the Hill is later involved in fighting against Jacobite rebels, as Tom is nearly involved in opposing the uprising of 1745.

The main point of the Man of the Hill's story is to provide an object lesson for Tom and for the reader which will show what damage life can inflict on any young man not endowed with a good degree of benevolence and spiritual resilience. Experience has turned the old man into a sour, myopic misanthrope. The epigraph of *Tom Jones,* we recall, is Horace's translation of the *Odyssey's* first words, *Mores hominum multorum vidit.* The Man of the Hill, though he has traveled all over Europe, has not really "seen the ways of many men" because he has eyes only for the universal knavery of mankind. Tom, on the contrary, argues with the old man, surely speaking for Fielding, that "nothing should be esteemed as characteristical of a species but what is to be found among the best and most perfect individuals of that species" (VIII, 15).

The way the old man's story is set into the frame of the novel's action provides a dramatic commentary on the moral and intellectual inadequacy of this recluse's misanthropy. The Man of the Hill enters and leaves the novel accompanied by violence: we first see him attacked by thieves, from whom Tom saves him, and we take leave of him sitting quietly with his gun while Tom dashes off to rescue Mrs. Waters from the murderous Northerton. Both framing episodes supply vivid evidence for the old man's dim view of humanity, but in each instance we also see one of the better examples of the species—Tom—performing a courageous act of spontaneous good will. The old man's misanthropy has induced in him a kind of moral paralysis, so that, when Mrs. Waters is attacked, he is incapable of the sort of humane action through which Tom saved his life a little earlier, and through which he himself rescued his father when he was a younger, and less bitter, man.

It should be noted, moreover, that this entire exploration through interpolation of the central subject of philanthropy and misanthropy, concluding with a general survey of human nature, occurs just before the halfway point of the novel. A moment before Tom is to leave the old man, at the beginning of Book IX (Chapter 2), which is to say, near the end of the first half of the novel, he looks out from the prominence of Mazard Hill and reminds us where we have come to: "Alas! sir . . . I was endeavouring to trace out my own journey hither. Good heavens! what a distance is Gloucester from us! What a vast track of land must be between me and my home." Here we have Fielding's Ulysses at midpoint between the journey out and the journey back, between the sunny security of Paradise Hall and the shadowy ways of devious London. It is altogether fitting that he should have just been exposed to a formal portrait in full length of what the world can do to a man who does not meet it squarely and judge it coolly but generously.

The interpolated tales, then, somewhat hesitantly in *Joseph Andrews* but emphatically in *Tom Jones,* are conceived as an integral part of the artistic scheme of the novel. As readers, we may feel that we pay too high a price for the elaboration of parallels and the contrast of narrative modes in losing for so many pages the engaging wittiness and stylistic complexity of Fielding's principal narrator: this is, clearly, an intrinsic and serious limitation of the interpolative method. It is important to see, however, that the juxtaposition of contrasting textures in the use of the interpolated stories is entirely at one with other procedures of Fielding's in the main body of the narrative.

He has a craftsman's sense of blocks of material which need to be deployed in aesthetically interesting patterns—for the most part, as we would expect, antithetical patterns. The discourse between the poet and the player in *Joseph Andrews* to which we referred a little earlier is introduced by the narrator's resolution to "imitate the wise conductors of the stage, who in the midst of a grave action entertain you with some excellent piece of satire or humour called a dance." Like the defense of the prefatory chapters in *Tom Jones* which it anticipates, this statement is both self-mocking and honestly informative. The dialogue between the two conceited scoundrels is neatly paralleled in structure and contrasted in tenor by the dialogue of the two good men in distress, Joseph and Adams, which immediately follows it, introduced as "a sort of counterpart to this [first dialogue]." Similarly, in *Tom Jones*, Squire Allworthy's grave sermon to Jenny Jones on the evils of sexual indulgence (I, 7) is immediately followed by a lively satiric dialogue between Bridget and Mrs. Wilkins, a sort of comic sermon in duet, in which the two spinsters vent their spleen on all loose wenches while Bridget, surprisingly, makes a generous exception for Jenny. Our attention is properly called to the contrasting blocks of material by the heading for Chapter 8: "A Dialogue Between Mesdames Bridget and Deborah Containing More Amusement, But Less Instruction, than the Former." As with other things in Fielding, this use of contrast can be inventive and unexpected, as here, or geometrically simple, like the chapter "Containing Two Letters in Very Different Styles" (XVIII, 4), which sets Square's sincere confession alongside the last self-seeking, snarling, back-biting words we hear from the Reverend Thwackum.

We have seen how Fielding works dull conventional stuff into the fabric of his novels to set off the richness, suppleness, and exquisite workmanship of his own stylistic and narrative brocade. This means that, as a rule, even the unnaturalness of actual dialogue or the strained quality of some of the narration has a purposeful function in the design of the novel.

I would like to offer one extended example of how this technique of contrast is put brilliantly to work. A good many critics have been unwilling to forgive Fielding for ruining the climactic lovers' reconciliation in *Tom Jones* by stuffing the mouths of both his hero and his heroine with the most unconscionable fustian. A careful reading of that dialogue, however, together with its abrupt conclusion, should make it clear that the fustian is quite intentional, in fact indispensable to Fielding's artistic purpose.

"Easy! Sophia, call not such an exulting happiness as mine by so cold a name. O! transporting thought! am I not assured that the blessed day will come, when I shall call you mine; when fears shall be no more; when I shall have that dear, that vast, that exquisite, ecstatic delight of making my Sophia happy?" "Indeed, sir," said she, "that day is in your own power." "O! my dear, divine angel," cried he, "these words have made me mad with joy.— But I must, I will thank those dear lips which have so sweetly pronounced my bliss." He then caught her in his arms, and kissed her with an ardour he had never ventured before.

At this instant Western, who had stood some time listening, burst into the room, and, with his hunting voice and phrase, cried out, "To her, boy, to her, go to her. That's it, little honeys, O, that's it. Well! what, is it all over? Hath she appointed the day, boy? What, shall it be to-morrow or next day? It shan't be put off a minute longer than next day, I am resolved." "Let me beseech you, sir," says Jones, "don't let me be the occasion—" "Beseech mine a____," cries Western. "I thought thou hadst been a lad of higher mettle than to give a way to a parcel of maidenish tricks. I tell thee 'tis all flimflam. Zoodikers! she'd have the wedding to-night with all her heart. Would'st not, Sophy? Come, confess, and be an honest girl for once. What, art dumb? Why dost not speak?" "Why should I confess, sir," says Sophia, "since it seems you are so well acquainted with my thoughts?" (XVIII, 12)

Now Tom Jones, as an examination of his speeches throughout the novel will reveal, has a latent streak of moralistic stuffiness running through all his buoyant insouciance and *joie de vivre;* it is, I suppose, an unfortunate side effect of Fielding's determination to make him an exemplary figure, however wayward. But Fielding has the sureness of novelistic instinct to exploit at certain important junctures the comic potential of his own hero's goodness. In this whole dialogue, Sophia has been turning about Tom in a coy minuet, he urgently pleading his own cause but fearful of being too forward, she out of wounded feminine pride and a sense of prudence keeping a cool distance, against her natural instincts. By this point, Tom has fallen altogether into the cadences and verbal formulas of the hero of a conventional romance —again Fielding makes us aware of the status of his novel as a literary artifact. The parade of exclamation points, the exulting happiness and transporting thoughts, the lapse of the prose into bad blank verse, the kiss "with an ardour he had never ventured before," are all conscious parody. I am in fact tempted to wonder whether Fielding had seen the newly published *Roderick Random* when he put the finishing touches to *Tom Jones.* In any event, it is just this kind of conventionally bad writing that Smollett reproduces in his heatedly overwrought, coldly underimagined account of the passion of Roderick for the fair Narcissa.

At the very moment when the lovers have become uncomfortably literary, "life" explodes upon the scene in the irresistible person of Squire Western, calling out to the lovers as he would to the hounds, urging Tom on in the pursuit of puss, dismissing a mannered hesitancy with the invocation of his a——, telling his daughter he knows just what she wants and how soon she would like to have it. Sophia's response, which confesses something of the artificiality of the preceding dialogue, is a stroke of poised double irony of the sort one scarcely finds in the English novel until Jane Austen. Sophia of course means to be ironic at her father's expense, though her indirection is obviously wasted on him, but what she admits with merely ironic intention she also knows to be quite true—that for once her father is very well acquainted with her unexpressed thoughts, that what she really wants is to be able to put aside Tom's past indiscretions and her own woman's pride, and hasten to bed with her lover.

Fielding's interest in contrasting parallels is by no means limited to verbal texture. The events of his plots are so arranged that the reader, if he possesses the requisite alertness, becomes aware of significant analogies, repetitions, and reversals in the fictional events themselves. In *Joseph Andrews* we can see this procedure put to work in a simple, but strikingly effective, way in the reiterated juxtaposition of Lady Booby's attempted seduction of Joseph and Mrs. Slipslop's uncommitted rape of that same unsuspecting figure. There are also more sustained symmetries of incident in this novel, but it will be more appropriate to consider them later in tracing the book's general unity of structure. "We hope," the narrator of *Joseph Andrews* tells us at the beginning of I, 7, "a judicious reader will give himself some pains to observe, what we have so greatly labored to describe, the different operations of this passion of love in the gentle and cultivated mind of the Lady Booby, from those which it effected in the less polished and coarser disposition of Mrs. Slipslop." It is not surprising that what the greatly laboring narrator in fact shows us is almost the opposite of this. While the strategies of attack of the two women differ—the lady extending coyly undraped arms to young Andrews and the servant preparing "to lay her violently amorous hands on the poor Joseph" (I, 6)—their minds are moved by the same raw female lust. Fielding himself makes the point nicely, in the deft seam stitch with which he concludes Chapter 6 and brings us back from the maid to the mistress, who "was left by Joseph in a temper of mind not greatly different from that of the inflamed Slipslop." The yoking of Lady Booby and Mrs. Slipslop could be thought of as a special satiric variation on the Quixote-

Sancho formula. Slipslop, in her assertively corpulent presence, is the vivid and unseemly embodiment of all the weaknesses that female flesh—including highborn female flesh—is heir to. With her abruptly outspoken manner, she is both a voice for and critic of the desires her mistress politely conceals, a living testimony to what lies on the other side of Lady Booby's facade of hypocrisy: " 'Do as I bid you,' says my lady, 'and don't shock my ears with your beastly language.' 'Marry-come-up,' cries Slipslop, 'people's ears are sometimes the nicest part about them' " (I, 9).

The juxtaposition, of course, of the would-be seductress and the frustrated female rapist is primarily a parallel of character, though it also involves a limited parallel of incident. In *Tom Jones,* on the other hand, where the whole plan of the novel is much more capacious and also much more intricately worked out, there are many suggestive repetitions of incident, sometimes with significant variations, that are not dependent upon the pairing of characters. Irvin Ehrenpreis has observed that the symmetrical structure of *Tom Jones* makes it possible for Fielding to set up similar scenes at opposite ends of the novel which can serve as didactic commentary upon one another. The examples he offers are Tom's averted duel with Northerton early in the book and his almost fatal duel with Fitzpatrick toward the end; Square's hiding behind the curtain in Molly's bedroom, and Lady Bellaston, then Lady Bellaston and Honour, behind the curtain in Tom's London bedroom; the early banishment of Tom, falsely accused, matched by the final banishment of Blifil, the deceiver unmasked.[5]

To these we might add Tom's discovery of Molly's amorous past in the first third of the novel and of Lady Bellaston's in the last third: in each case, he has imagined himself engaged by honor to the woman with whom he slept, but he learns that Molly was happily "corrupted" long before he enjoyed her favors, and Nightingale informs him of Lady Bellaston that "you are not the first young fellow she has debauched"

(XV, 9). In a symmetry of incident that has a middlepoint as well, Squire Western urges men on like hounds in pursuit of the slippery female early in the novel, when Molly is hiding in the bushes; near the beginning of the middle third, when Blifil is making his odious advances to Sophia; and, as we have seen, at the end, when with Tom and Sophia the impetuous master of the hunt at last finds the true hound and the true fox.

There are other ingenious recurrences or reversals of incident which are not placed at opposite ends of the novel. In Chapter 6 of the first book, Jenny Jones, who one day will share Tom's bed and who is about to confess herself mother of another woman's bastard, rouses the envious wrath of the whole female community by appearing in church in a fine silk gown. A little later (IV, 7 and 8), Molly Seagrim, who has already had relations with Tom and whose belly is beginning to bulge with her own bastard, is actually assaulted by the women of the parish for coming to church in a cast-off lady's gown—given her, in fact, by the woman who has sole possession of Tom's heart and will one day have the rest of him, too. Tom, we recall, arrives just in time to rescue Molly from this graveyard onslaught; later he himself will be assaulted by Thwackum and Blifil for heading into the bushes with Molly; and, still further on, he will rescue Jenny Jones as she is being homicidally assaulted in a lonely wood. The motives for the attack, and its objects, shift, but the various attackers resemble each other in the impulse of spiteful malice upon which they act.

The cunningly contrived recurrences of incident, it should be clear, help create an awareness of moral continuities within the novel; as with so many other strategies of Fielding's, their function is integrative, leading us to relate individual characters and their actions to other characters and other circumstances. The aim of the variations on a single action is not to imply simple equations but, as in the case of the coyly ironic style, to tease us into thought about analogies. When, for example, Mrs. Waters is discovered in bed with Tom Jones, she adopts a role which, as we later learn, is a neat reversal of the one she played at the beginning of the novel: as Jenny Jones, she assumed the guilt of a sexual indiscretion she never committed; now, in the very warmth of the bed of pleasure, she feigns innocence with desperate cries of "Help! Rape! Murder!" This leads the narrator to make one of his indispensable generalizations: "And hence, I think, we may very fairly draw an argument to prove how extremely natural virtue is to the fair sex; for though there is not, perhaps, one in ten thousand who is capable of making a good actress . . . this [character] of virtue they can all admirably well put on" (X, 2). The observation invites us to compare Mrs. Waters protesting her virtue with Bridget and Mrs. Wilkins, those two good spinsters so remarkable for the chastity of their ears; later, we are given occasion to recall this general "argument" drawn from Mrs. Waters' action when we see the transparent pretense to innocence of Mrs. Fitzpatrick and Lady Bellaston.

Repetition may be used to make us refer a whole series of events to a single moral generalization, as in this case, or, more diagrammatically, to bring out a broad contrast, as in the double correspondence of marriage proposals in which Tom is involved (XV, 9 and 11). Tom's letter asking for the hand of Lady Bellaston is pure stratagem contrived for a woman who deserves nothing better: it achieves its aim, though it will complicate Tom's relationship with Sophia in a still unguessed way, when milady calls Tom a villain and warns him not to see her again. Set back to back with this proposal, separated only by the thin buffer of Chapter 10—which, incidentally, contains another sort of letter, Honour's wonderfully illiterate note to Tom—is the correspondence between Mrs. Hunt and Tom. In the latter exchange, Tom is the object of a most sincere and decent proposal from the well-to-do young widow: the fact of the proposal is a testimony to his personal merit and his tactfully frank refusal is evidence of his honest loyalty to Sophia, so that we see immediate demonstrations that he is worthy of Sophia, just when he has rid himself of the woman in whose keeping he was. In the juxtaposition, moreover, of the two very different proposals and refusals, we are clearly shown the startling distance between the coldly selfish hedonism and dishonesty of Lady Bellaston's fashionable London world, from which Tom is now emerging unscathed, and the reassuring openness of modest, honest people who have not been alienated from their own human feelings by a relentless pursuit of pleasure and prestige. One may feel that the social and moral antithesis implicit in the contrasting proposals is excessively neat, but in the comic scheme of the novel it provides a useful transition from the sophisticated sphere of pretense to the atmosphere of candor and reconciliation in which all the comic difficulties will finally be resolved.

The most cunningly conceived repetitions of incident in *Tom Jones* are those which not only suggest instructive comparisons but also form intricate links in the concatenation of the plot. A fairly simple example is the double discovery of lost banknotes, Tom's, which is appropriated by Black George, and Sophia's, which Tom keeps faithfully to restore to her. Both actions fit with nice significance into the London complications of the plot. The same technique is made to work with greater moral subtlety in two instances of related munificence, Lady Bellaston's generosity to Tom and Tom's to poor Mr. Anderson. The second of these actions, reported in "A Chapter Which, Though Short, May Draw Tears from Some Eyes" (XIII, 10), is one of those occasional points in Fielding where even enthusiastic readers may begin to feel uneasy. The incident, which looks across to the dewy-eyed passages in Smollett and forward to the sentimental scenes in Dickens, is obviously contrived to prove with a vengeance that Tom is a Good Man with a Good Heart and that no act is more rewarding than an act of benevolence. "Oh, you are an excellent young man," Mrs. Miller cries out to Tom in a characteristic access of simpering gratitude, and one almost wishes Fielding had spiced her saccharine goodness by making her a bawd on the side.

If the scene as whole, with its flood of blessings on the virtuous head of Jones, is a sentimental simplification of novelistic facts, an element of complexity is introduced through the ironic parallel between Tom's act of generosity and Lady Bellaston's, of which we are informed just a little earlier (XIII, 8). Lest it be thought I am imposing a parallel where one barely exists, I would like to point out that Fielding takes pains in his elaborate irony to present as a nobly philanthropic gesture the lady's payment for services rendered:

> To clear, therefore, the honour of Mr. Jones, and to do justice to the liberality of the lady, he had really received this present of her, who, though she did not give much into the hackney charities of the age, such as building hospitals, etc., was not, however, entirely void of that Christian virtue; and conceived (very rightly, I think) that a young fellow of merit, without a shilling in the world, was no improper object of this virtue.

The sentence is a fine example of how satiric irony in Fielding flows into psychology: the devastating exposure of the moral coarseness in an aging lady who hires her lovers catches what must certainly be the polite rationalization by which she justifies her own actions to herself. More to our present purpose, this ironic assumption of charitable motives prepares us to link Lady Bellaston's generosity with Tom's, when in the same chapter he volunteers £50 to the unknown kinsman of Mrs. Miller, who, two chapters later, turns out to be the unfortunate Mr. Anderson. We have scarcely had time to forget that Tom's genuinely benevolent action depends upon one of Lady Bellaston's which is only ostensibly that: the money he gives to save an indigent family from starvation is the money he has received from an amorous lady for saving her from frustration.

The faculty for making connections so essential to Fielding's narrative method here raises a nice moral question as well as affirming a moral judgment: is an act of goodness in any way compromised by depending upon a dishonorable act, or, on the other hand, may a moral lapse be rectified, retroactively, as it were, by a palpable benefaction that follows from it? This kind of delicate weighing of moral imponderables, however, requires a more finely analytic fictional vehicle—say, Henry James's—for any elaborate development, and Fielding does not pursue the point. What he does emphasize in Tom's joyful meeting with the Andersons is the bold moral contrast between his sincere altruism and Lady Bellaston's worldly sensualism.

"If, by the trifle you have received from me," Tom tells Mr. Anderson, "I have preserved a whole family, sure pleasure was never bought so cheap." The emphasis on buying pleasure cheap is no chance turn of phrase. Tom's benevolence is carefully presented in terms of a kind of Christian hedonism, an instance of the highest, and the most gratifying, pleasure, which only a virtuous soul can enjoy. Tom goes on to point the moral: "If there are men who cannot feel the delight of giving happiness to others, I sincerely pity them, as they are incapable of tasting what is, in my opinion, a greater honour, a higher interest, and a sweeter pleasure than the ambitious, the avaricious, or the voluptuous man can ever obtain." As novelistic dialogue, the oratorical cadences of Tom's speech, with the two balanced series of three terms, are stiffly unnatural, but the symmetrical formality of the language helps Fielding make the proper moral connections firmly. The categories Tom applies to men with no benevolent instinct effectively embrace all the villains and villainous acts of the novel, and they apply with particular pointedness to Lady Bellaston, whose life is wholly preoccupied, in ascending order of preference, with honor, interest, and sweet pleasure.

The narrator also introduces here what looks very much like a comparison in Tom's favor with Squire Allworthy. For the young benefactor of the Andersons pauses a moment to reflect on the catastrophe he would have caused had he, when attacked on the highway by the desperate pater familias, "listened rather to the voice of strict justice than to that of mercy." This is, of course, precisely what Allworthy, good man that he is, does more than once in the first part of the novel, through just this lack of lenient judgment setting the machinery of the main plot in motion. Perhaps Tom is not the only virtuous character who has something to learn in the course of the novel.

Because Fielding is so concerned with conveying moral meanings through his comedy, one of the most sustained unities of his novels is thematic. Virtually all of the action and dialogue, as well as the authorial comment, refers to one or another of a set of interrelated moral themes, and, as we have seen in another connection, actual verbal motifs are used to make the thematic development more explicit. This kind of unity obtains as much in *Joseph Andrews*, where the series of narrated incidents is in part episodic, as it does in *Tom Jones*, where there is a strict causal sequence in the plot. A number of central themes are common to both novels, simply because Fielding assumes the same general moral topography in both books and so quite naturally invokes the same formal categories for organizing moral experience, but the kind of emphasis given to the themes changes.

Thus both novels, as we have had more than one occasion to note, make repeated reference to the contrast of town and country, the town representing the sophisticated degeneracy of modern life, and the country, though it harbors the expected varieties of vanity and knavery, holding within it a possibility of a decent traditional life in the small Christian community of family and friends. In *Joseph Andrews*, however, this contrast is given more prominence, at least in the initial and concluding sections, because the entire action of the novel is a broad movement from London and separation to the final discovery and union in the country. In the early chapters, therefore, we encounter repeated allusions to the vain frivolity of the town, to the country as seen by the town, and to the town as seen by the country (in the person of Joseph). Lady Booby, "who had been blest with a town education . . . never spoke of any of her country neighbours by any other appellation than that of 'the Brutes' " (I, 3). Joseph's fellow servants try to introduce him to the fashions of the town, which, in addition to foppish attire, consist of swearing, drinking, gaming, rioting at playhouses and assemblies, and similar "genteel vices" (I, 4). Since the novel will culminate in the classic comic establishment of a true community, Joseph pronounces the most telling judgment on the town in suggesting that it isolates men from one another: "London is a bad place, and there is so little good fellowship that the next-door neighbours don't know one another" (I, 7). At the other end of the novel, when all the characters converge on Lady Booby's estate, Beau Didapper is introduced to serve as an embodiment of the quintessence of the town in the midst of the country. The conjunction of the beau in his laced velvet finery and Parson Adams in his rusty cassock, each mocking the other's garb, is a sharply focused satiric image of the whole opposition of town and country.

One of the most important themes of *Joseph Andrews*, which we have also touched on before, is the shifting meaning of the term "Christian," often mentioned in contrast to Turks, Jews, and other infidels. As the true pastor Abraham Adams and the loyal disciple Joseph together with his beloved make their pilgrim's progress through a land of deceivers (see, for

example, the nighttime march in III, 2, which is, paradigmatically, the perilous journey of a faithful band in a dark
world), the word "Christian" is on every tongue, including
some that look suspiciously forked.

Most of the characters are inclined to define as a true Christian whoever can best serve their self-interest, or whoever
makes use of the means of power they themselves most readily
employ. A gentleman volunteering legal advice to Adams
after his battle with the Towwouses suggests that "if your jury
were Christians, they must give swinging damages" (II, 5).
When Adams tells Trulliber, the pig-farming parson, that
"Whoever is void of charity . . . is no Christian," his uncouth
brother to the cloth responds with a rather different definition
of a Christian: "I would not advise thee . . . to say that I
am no Christian; I won't take it of you; for I believe I am
as good a man as thyself." This Christian goodness he then
prepares to demonstrate with the might of his two fists. The
fawning Mrs. Trulliber, on the other hand, has still another
notion of what a Christian is: "His wife, seeing him clench
his fist, interposed, and begged him not to fight, but show
himself a true Christian, and take the law of him" (II, 14).
In contrast to such self-deluding hypocrisy, the huntsman in
charge of the hounds that attacked Adams is refreshingly candid
when he points out the essential undesirability of Christians
as objects of the chase: "He . . . wondered his master would
encourage the dogs to hunt *Christians* . . . it was the surest
way to spoil them, to make them follow *vermin* instead of
sticking to the hare" (III, 6). It is easy to sympathize with
the good parson when he fears he will be thought no Christian
for lack of gold in his pocket, or because of the shabbiness
of his clothes; and his protestation of innocence, when in the
great climax of bedroom confusions he is found in Fanny's bed,
resonates marvelously against all the accumulated uses of this
central thematic term: "As I am a Christian, I know not
whether she is a man or woman" (IV, 14). These words,

which literally echo others of Joseph's to Lady Booby early in the novel (I, 8), state a finely ironic truth, for Adams' indisputable Christian innocence is inseparable from his unworldliness, from his being scarcely aware of those powerful facts of difference between man and woman.

Parson Adams in general, and, more particularly, Parson Adams in Fanny's bed, suggests another set of mutually related themes around which *Joseph Andrews* is shaped—appearance and reality, clothing and nakedness. Mark Spilka has shown quite effectively how the development of these particular themes comes to a brilliantly comic culmination in the bedroom farce at Lady Booby's,[6] though he tends, I think, to insist on an explicitness of symbolic signification which Fielding himself does not really suggest. There can hardly be "a definite symbolic equation between nakedness, on the one hand, and innocence and worth, on the other," when the first instance of nakedness in the novel is that of Lady Booby! Fielding is coy, full of dialectical reversals, in his "symbolic equations" as in his ironic double meanings. In part, nakedness is the image he uses in *Joseph Andrews* for the human thing itself, stripped, as we say, of all disguise.

Lady Booby's nakedness is the visual revelation of the naked lust she can scarcely conceal. When Joseph is dismissed from her service, our attention is pointedly drawn to the fact that he is "stripped" of his livery: his vestments having been removed in a kind of rite of passage, he abandons the role he played at the Boobys' and returns to his own world. He is soon stripped again, by the highwaymen who assault him and leave him for dead. In this case, the nakedness emphasizes not so much innocence as helpless vulnerability, the starkest image of need for Christian charity. The various responses of the stagecoach passengers, on the other hand, to the naked man on the road do express a decided lack of innocence—false prudery, smirking delight in the possibilities of sexual embarrassment, self-interested unwillingness to contemplate the bare forked thing that calls for their help. Elsewhere, Joseph's fine white skin elicits a good deal of admiring comment from the women in the novel: apart from reminding us of his physical attractiveness, it serves as a social rather than a moral index, giving us fair intimation that he is in fact, as we finally learn, a proper gentleman. In a ceremony of transition which balances the stripping of livery early in the novel, Joseph toward the end of the book is dressed in fine gentleman's clothes by his supposed brother-in-law Booby (IV, 5), and we see at last how the texture of cloth matches the texture of the skin, Joseph, a sort of male Cinderella, now revealed to the world as his true self.

Conversely, people concerned with creating appearances rather than confronting realities are preoccupied with clothing. The most extreme example is Beau Didapper, whose foppishness is the chief expression of his impotent pursuit of vice: the slave of appearances, he is quite content to possess the mere reputation of intrigues he is unable to carry out. Much attention is given to dress in the Booby household; Adams tells us that he ceased to be invited there because the lady thought his attire not good enough for the gentry at her table (II, 8). Mr. Wilson confesses that, at the beginning of his moral decline in London, he sought to attain the character of a fine gentleman, "the first requisites to which I apprehended were to be supplied by a tailor" (III, 3). In such a world, it is no wonder that Adams' defense of the Christian pastor, "who clothes you with piety," is answered with an innkeeper's taunt, "I do not remember ever to have seen any such clothing" (II, 17); and the prelapsarian truth that "a man naturally wants clothes no more than a horse" comes from the smug mouth of Peter Pounce, as an excuse for not giving charity (III, 13).

Against this whole background, it is finely appropriate that the two lovers should refuse all elaborate dress on their wedding day, wearing instead clothes that are at once simple in appearance and fine in quality, and that Fanny's preparations for the final consummation of the marriage are described in the following terms: "Undressing to her was properly discovering, not putting off, garments: for, as all her charms were the gifts of nature, she could divest herself of none." In view of the whole development of nakedness and clothing as formal themes in the novel, this is a beautifully precise statement. Fanny's nakedness is indeed innocence, for that is her inner nature, and so disrobing is merely the perfect revelation of her own honest and lovely self; but nakedness has other implications in other characters because their natures are different from hers.

In the case of Beau Didapper and Madame Slipslop, in fact, which Parson Adams so hilariously mistakes, nakedness itself presents a deceptive appearance, not a reality. One wonders whether here, too, Fielding may have had a biblical model at least in the back of his mind. In Genesis, the son and grandson of the parson's biblical namesake are both deceived by the sense of touch in the dark, one about the identity of his firstborn, the other about his bride; in Slipslop's bedroom we have, as it were, an Abraham feeling the hands of Esau which are attached to the sex of Leah.

Other significant encounters occur in the dark, which is hardly surprising in a novel designed to show the moral necessity of distinguishing between seeming and being. Parson Adams first comes upon Fanny in the black of the night, at the moment she is being assaulted, as is her wont, by a lustful man. Without recognizing her, without, in fact, the opportunity to see any appearances in the dark, only hearing a woman's screams for help, he rushes to her rescue in a purely unmeditated impulse of humanity (II, 9). When, having vanquished the assailant, he and Fanny are accosted by the nocturnal bird hunters, the two good souls appear very different from what they are in the illusory light of the hunters' lantern: Fanny's hair is disheveled and her nose bleeding, while the parson, in the unanimous opinion of the hunters, "had the most villainous countenance they had ever beheld" (II, 10). This is, by the way, not the only reference to physiognomy in the novel; ironically, a little later it is Parson Adams who comes to the defense of that dubious science, passionately insisting that the reality can be judged on the basis of the appearance (II, 17). From this last episode, it should again be clear that even in the passages that look like mere diversions—in this case a long dialogue on sundry matters between Adams and an innkeeper—the thematic development of the novel is firmly supported. A parallel episode to Adams' meeting with Fanny in the dark is the scene in which he, Fanny, and Joseph discover the eerily flickering lights and hear the grim descriptions of slaughter of a desperate group that turn out to be mere sheep thieves (III, 2). The incident, obviously patterned on the adventure of the fulling mills in *Don Quixote*, provides still another comic illustration of the deceptiveness of appearances.

Mr. Wilson, whose story in general is intended to make didactically explicit what is merely suggested in the surrounding narrative, sums up this opposition between appearance and reality in his reflections on his early experiences with the women of London. After absorbing his third dose of the clap from the town whores, this is the way he learned to see them: "Their persons appeared to me as painted palaces, inhabited by Disease and Death: nor could their beauty make them more desirable objects in my eyes than gilding could make me covet a pill, or golden plates a coffin." And a moment later, he says of the more fashionable coquettes of the town that "the only rule by which you can form any judgment of them is, that they are never what they seem" (III, 3). This is didactic, indeed; we are likely to feel happier about Fielding when he is, in more typical fashion, comically inventive in varying his themes.

In any event, Fielding's thematic continuities are hardly an instrument for the discovery of subtleties. He may be said to elaborate his themes more often than he actually develops them. What he does with his themes, finally, is to work them through his narrative materials as formal elements in an ingenious pattern of repetition and variation that contributes to the novel's intellectual coherence and structural strength. Fielding's themes obviously appeal to the intellect, in contrast to later novelists like Conrad and Mann whose use of themes appeals primarily to the imagination; but it is an intellect confident of what it already knows, ready to enjoy in the new narrative art of the novelist "Nature to advantage dressed,/ What oft was thought, but ne'er so well expressed."

All the themes we have been considering in *Joseph Andrews*, with the exception of the concept "Christian," also play important parts in *Tom Jones*. But in the longer novel, the themes are somewhat less conspicuous, perhaps because the more tautly drawn narrative skein tends to lead our attention away from the explicit moral design to the bustle and excitement of what is happening and to the personages who make it happen. The themes of clothing and nakedness, appearance and reality, are integrated in *Tom Jones* with the theme of masks which they virtually imply. Tom's real induction into London life occurs at a masquerade: it is there he joins company with Lady Bellaston, whose true identity he does not guess, and she, in the most significant of synecdoches, is referred to by the narrator as "the mask" (XIII, 7). (In *Amelia*, for reasons we shall consider later, Fielding makes the masquerade even more central than this in the structure of his novel.) In the prefatory chapter to Book XIII, the very book in which the masquerade is reported, Fielding makes clear what was already implicit in *Joseph Andrews*, that his most basic procedure as a novelist is an act of laying bare, of unmasking: "Teach me," he invokes his Genius, "to know mankind better than they know themselves . . . Strip off the thin disguise of wisdom from self-conceit, of plenty from avarice, and of glory from ambition."

There is no need to chase after all the agile play with these themes in *Tom Jones:* it does not differ in kind from the varied applications of theme which we have already followed out in *Joseph Andrews.* But if there is no significant technical innovation in the thematic aspect of *Tom Jones,* Fielding uses the technique with a masterly suppleness and easy precision not evident to the same degree in the earlier novel, and integrates it more completely into his whole narrative method. Through his extraordinarily deft handling of themes in *Tom Jones,* he shows what resources of coherent and exact expression are made available by the architectonic novel he invented. Individual passages are supported lightly but firmly by the weight of the entire novel, benefiting from the structural strengths and shapeliness of the whole.

When the narrator gives us a character of Lady Bellaston, by way of explaining and judging Tom's liaison with her, the architectonics of the total work inform the passage. Details of this particular portrait fall together in an easy unity that recalls the larger thematic patterns of the novel.

Such was the unhappy case of Jones; for though the virtuous love he bore Sophia, and which left very little affection for any other woman, had been entirely out of the question, he could never have been able to have made any adequate return to the generous passion of this lady, who had indeed been once an object of desire, but was now entered at least into the autumn of life, though she wore all the gayety of youth, both in her dress and manner; nay, she contrived still to maintain the roses in her cheeks; but these, like flowers forced out of season by art, had none of that lively blooming freshness with which Nature, at the proper time, bedecks her own productions. She had, besides, a certain imperfection which renders some flowers, though very beautiful to the eye, very improper to be placed in a wilderness of sweets, and what above all others is most disagreeable to the breath of love. (XIII, 9)

The passage is a beautiful example of Fielding's devastatingly decorous irony, from its pointed pun on the "generosity" of the lady's passion to the last elegant allusion to her stinking breath, in which the narrator's hand, as it moves to hold his nose, is covered with a stylistic kid glove of the finest fashion. But this is much more than an isolated piece of ingenious irony. The figure of Lady Bellaston, as it is fixed for inspection, is intersected by most of the major thematic vectors of the novel. She "wears" all the gaiety of youth in overblown middle age—just as Bridget, after the death of her husband, "dressed her person and countenance" in the appropriate colors of sadness (II, 9)—and so we immediately see her in terms of the recurrent disparity between clothing and nakedness, mask and man (or woman), appearance and reality. This series of thematic oppositions is directly related to still another polarity—art and nature. The last two terms, which were the focal points for so much discussion throughout the Renaissance, are usually an underlying concern in *Tom Jones,* and occasionally, as in the episodes of the puppet show, of Partridge at the theater, of the gypsy wedding, they receive direct treatment. Nature in Fielding is of course good, is in fact the ultimate source of all positive values, but it generally needs the intelligent restraint of art—prudence is surely a kind of art, devoted to the creation of proper moral appearances. Art without nature, on the other hand, is a monstrosity; Lady Bellaston is all art and contrivance, herself a hothouse flower impiously cultivated out of season with the most indecent manures. In this way, a simple physical fact—that this faded beauty rouges her cheeks—is related through metaphor to theme and so made to refer precisely and persuasively to a large framework of moral assessment.

At the beginning of the passage, moreover, we are invited to compare Tom's artful, aging mistress with Sophia, who is young, naturally beautiful, and naturally sweet, whose only contrivances are the minimal ones required by a healthy feminine pride and a sense of reasonable social propriety. The "little affection for any other woman" which Jones has left after his love for Sophia may also make us think of the other two women with whom he is unfaithful to Sophia: Tom's sexual generosity, we see, has been leading him progressively farther away from unadorned nature—from Molly Seagrim, the plain country flower whose stenches are all of the barnyard variety, to Mrs. Waters, a somewhat more sophisticated roadside blossom, which does not come under olfactory examination in the novel, and now to Lady Bellaston, the subtle hothouse growth that gives off the gamy odor of imminent decay.

It is a matter of conjecture whether Fielding consciously contrived every one of his details to dovetail in the way I have been describing. At the very least, we must assume that the unity of design which he clearly envisaged had become so much a part of his imagination that he could allude to it almost without thinking, in the most casual observations, the art of the novel having become second nature to the novelist.

The presence of these particular continuities in both of Fielding's comic novels should by now be amply apparent; what remains to be seen is how the action as a whole falls into a unified pattern. In this respect, *Tom Jones* has been the subject of considerable critical discussion and admiration, but *Joseph Andrews* deserves more attention than it has received.[7] The old view of Fielding's first novel as a parody of *Pamela* that by happy accident galloped away on its own course has been pretty well discredited in recent years; I would like to show that *Joseph Andrews* is given shape not only by the elaboration of themes and the counterposing of contrasted narrative materials but also by an embracing architectonic conception. Admittedly, some of the particular actions, especially in the two middle books, are episodic—others might conceivably be substituted for them or, occasionally, their order could be transposed. Yet even if the causal progression of the action is sometimes sketchy, the whole narrative is blocked out through the four books in a balanced pattern which, in the artful coherence of its formal symmetries, looks almost like a novelistic premonition of the form of the classical symphony.

After the necessary exposition at the beginning of the first book (Chapters 1 through 4), the main action begins with Lady Booby's first effort to seduce Joseph, and thus a recurrent situation, the attempted sexual violation of an innocent, and a major theme, chastity, are introduced. Book I in fact offers us a small social panorama of sexually aggressive women, beginning with Lady Booby, the sexual hypocrite, moving down the social scale and up the moral one to Slipslop, the maid-in-waiting who is at times almost honest about her lust, and concluding, still lower socially and higher morally, with Betty the chambermaid, in whom physical desire is associated with a generosity of mind as well as of body. A little over halfway through the book, when Joseph is found naked on the road and is finally taken up by the postilion, a second major theme, charity, is stated for the first time. Further on, as Joseph resists seduction by Betty after benefiting from her kind and disinterested ministrations, the themes of chastity and charity are brought together. The formal symmetry of the book is reinforced by the actions at the beginning and the very end: first we see Joseph expelled from his servant's position for having repulsed the advances of Lady Booby; at the end, Betty, in the heat of having been repulsed by Joseph, easily yields to the advances of her employer, and when she is caught in the act by her mistress, she, too, is turned away from her place.

In Books II and III the modes of action and dialogue tend to be discursive, in contrast to Books I and IV, where they are more continually dramatic. This textural contrast, however, does not imply any loosening of structure. Book II begins with Parson Adams on the road absorbed in the contemplation of his Aeschylus, at one point seated on a stile, totally unaware, because he has not raised his eyes from his book, that the inn he seeks is a hundred yards away. This memorable

image of Adams, unaware of his immediate surroundings because of his absorption in learning, is an apt preface to a
whole series of encounters in roadside inns and over the
countryside in which he finds that men are not what they
seem to be, in which there is an unsettling disparity between
appearance and reality. A little over halfway through this
book, Fanny enters the novel, like Joseph, as the object of
sexual assault: Adams' valorous rush to her aid again joins
the themes of charity and chastity–lust. The book concludes with
a debate between Adams and the innkeeper on whether realities
can be inferred from appearances: this exchange looks back
on the immediately preceding episode of the pretended philan-
thropist, where the themes of appearance–reality and charity
are united, and prepares for the initial episode of the next
book, the nocturnal meeting with the sheep killers, in which
the opposition of appearance and reality is given a sharp
comic focus.

The third book, like the second, begins with Adams sitting
out in the open, now without his Aeschylus, but once again,
by virtue of the dark night, unaware of what is around him—
in this case, the two lovers, clasped in each other's arms a
little distance away. Book III introduces another threat to
Fanny's virginity; then it, too, ends with a "dialogue"—Fielding
uses the word in the headings for the final chapters of both
II and III—involving Parson Adams, this time with Peter
Pounce, on the question of charity. That central theme has
been sounded in several of the episodes of the two middle
books; it is particularly important in Book III because the
major action there, the attack on Adams by the hounds followed by the various conspiracies against him and his friends
by the malicious squire, is such a clear antithesis to the charitable aid and hospitality that should be proffered to afflicted
Christians.

Book IV, dispensing with a prefatory chapter as the narrative pace quickens, begins with the "second appearance of

Lady Booby on the stage," still smoldering with unsated lust, still accompanied by that crude reflection of her own desires, the outspoken and misspoken Slipslop. Another of Parson Adams' "dialogues," here with Lady Booby, is used at the beginning of the book as a structural overlap or seam to bind this last book with the two previous ones, each of which concluded with a dialogue. But as the narrative returns to a more strictly dramatic mode, the dialogue here involves no expatiation on general moral theory, only a confrontation of personalities over the practical question at hand—whether Fanny should be allowed to marry Joseph. The narrative now hurries through a cumulative series of comic threats to poor Fanny's virtue, finally to arrive at the happy goal of a true lovers' marriage; in the process, most of the major themes of the novel are recapitulated and the central comic situations restated. The grand bedroom scramble at Lady Booby's, in which many a sheet is rumpled but never a maidenhead cracked, is the culmination of all the thwarted assaults on virtue in the novel as well as a hilarious revelation of the most peculiar disparities between appearance and reality. In the two concluding chapters, we learn that Joseph is really what he appears to be, a gentleman and the providential mate for Fanny; and as the lovers at last enjoy the rewards of their constancy, "rewards so great and sweet . . . that Joseph neither envied the noblest duke, nor Fanny the finest duchess, that night," we come to the final, fitting reversal of those frustrated attempts by Lady Booby to seduce Joseph which initiated the main action.

The intricate unity of *Tom Jones,* which inspired Coleridge to call its plot one of the three most perfect in literature, is a matter of common critical knowledge, and the various formal aspects of that novel are so intimately linked with one another that we have already, necessarily, touched on most of them—the "geographical" division into three groups of six books each, paralleled by the triad of Tom's mistresses, the symmetrical recurrence of incidents at opposite ends of the novel, the balanced contrasts of town and country, the elaborate pairings of characters and events. The whole novel, in fact, can also be divided more or less neatly in half, with the action in many of the first nine books ingeniously answering to the action of the corresponding books in the second group of nine. It would be tedious for us to rehearse all of these (as Fielding himself surely would have said); in any event, simple repetition is resisted by Fielding frequently enough so that the parallels should not be mechanically obtrusive. I would, however, like to suggest a few of the clearer instances of correspondence.

In Book IV both Sophia and Molly are introduced and in Book V we are given the account of Sophia and Tom falling in love. In the fourth book of the second nine, Lady Bellaston is introduced; the subsequent book reports the establishment of her liaison with Tom. Sophia is harassed about Blifil by her aunt and father and then confined in Books VI and VII, as she is again in XV and XVI. Tom is wounded by the brawling Northerton in Book VII, as a consequence of which he is confined to bed and his assailant to a makeshift guardhouse; in Book XVI he wounds Fitzpatrick in a duel, resulting in his assailant's confinement in bed under surgeon's care and his own commitment to a prison cell. Book IX ends with Tom in the eager embrace of Mrs. Waters, whom he will later suppose to be his mother; Book XVIII culminates, after removing the doubts of incest and unraveling all the Upton entanglements, with Tom in bed at last with his beloved Sophia. In the second chapter of this last book, the narrator calls particular attention both to the cunning contrivance of the whole plot and to the way events in the ninth book reverberate in the eighteenth:

> If the reader will please to refresh his memory, turning to the scene at Upton, in the ninth book, he will be apt to admire the many strange accidents which unfortunately prevented any interview be-

tween Partridge and Mrs. Waters, when she spent a whole day there with Mr. Jones. Instances of this kind we may frequently observe in life, where the greatest events are produced by a nice train of little circumstances; and more than one example of this may be discovered by the accurate eye, in this our history.

This statement aptly suggests the connection between the elaborate clockwork mechanism of the plot and the significant symmetries of structure in *Tom Jones*. The narrator claims that the "nice train of little circumstances" is an observable phenomenon of causation in life itself, but at the same time he makes clear that his "history" is conscious artifice, divided into staged scenes and numbered books, regarded with a craftsman's pride by its contriver. The concatenation of minute events of the plot is an imitation of nature, but a comically heightened imitation; it is just this comic heightening of causation, pointing toward the burlesque of a philosophic issue, which Sterne picked up and brilliantly pushed to its extreme, as he did with other aspects of Fielding. The plot of *Tom Jones*, then, serves not only to generate comic suspense through the long reaches of an expansive narrative, but also to remind us of the presence of an artist, ordering the materials of life in a tight interconnection that actual experience only sometimes approximates, avoiding through a choice of comic art the incoherencies, the undispelled moral confusions, the irreversible calamities, which so abound in life.

In *Joseph Andrews*, Fielding worked out the guiding principles for the new literary form of which he saw himself as the innovator, that "comic epic poem in prose," a designation which he would playfully telescope in his subsequent novel (V, 1) into "prosai-comi-epic writing" in order to introduce the proper tincture of self-mocking facetiousness into his serious literary theory. In *Tom Jones* Fielding elaborated and expanded the method of *Joseph Andrews*, applying it with a new technical sureness and imaginative mastery, genuinely enlarging the smallest aspects of the novel by making them part of a more intricately architectonic whole. Although the frequent effect of his genial narrator was to make that which was beautifully planned and articulated seem like mere happy improvisation, his major work was nevertheless a consummate demonstration of what a writer could do if he took the novel seriously as an art form.

In succeeding generations of novelists, however, no one, with the exception of Sterne in his idiosyncratic way, was able to learn this lesson from Fielding. The artistic integrity, the inviolable unity of design, of his masterpiece were not generally perceived, and so writers tended to take from him mere isolated elements—the chatty narrator, the flights into the mock-sublime, the facetious chapter headings, the discovery of rightful heirs and the union of true lovers at the end— which, isolated and imitated, were rarely more than cheap, facile, and tedious devices.

In terms of Fielding's own career, he had written out his conception of the comic novel, for himself at any rate, realizing its best possibilities in the best way: after one *Tom Jones,* there could be no other. In his next work of fiction, therefore, he tried to create a new kind of novel, building in a different way on the base he had established in his two previous efforts in the genre. *Amelia* has to be seen, I think, as a transitional book, and as such, it repays close consideration for any student of fiction. Fate in Fielding's life, however, was less benign than Fortune in his great novel: dead at the age of forty-seven, less than three years after the publication of *Amelia,* he would never have the chance to take the next step in his progress as an artist.

*Fellows like Fielding . . . who pretend
that if you are a gay drunkard, lecher,
squanderer of your goods and fumbler in
placket-holes you will eventually find a
benevolent uncle, concealed father or
benefactor who will shower on you bags
of tens of thousands of guineas, estates and
the hands of adorable mistresses—those
fellows are dangers to the body-politic
and horribly bad constructors of plots.*
—*Ford Madox Ford,* The English Novel

5. FIELDING'S PROBLEM NOVEL

Fielding's last work of fiction can be thought of as a problem
novel in much the same way that the troubled comedies of
Shakespeare's middle period are often regarded as problem
plays. One gets a disconcerting sense that the tone of the writing is not always fully under the writer's control, and the
whole fiction threatens at times to slip down between the two
literary stools on which it is precariously perched. John Coolidge is surely right in attributing much of the artistic uncertainty of *Amelia* to a vacillation between the old manner of
Tom Jones and a new novelistic manner toward which Fielding
was groping with only an intuitive sense of direction.[1] I do
not think, though, that all the peculiar ambiguities of *Amelia*
can be explained through that formula, and it seems to me
important to get a clear notion at the outset of precisely what
Fielding meant to accomplish in his last novel.

Knowledge of the literary model Fielding had in mind is
helpful in this case, not because it can really serve as a
guide to reading *Amelia,* but because it suggests the tenor of

Fielding's intentions. Fielding himself, in the *Covent-Garden Journal* for January 28, 1752, called attention to his use of Virgil as the "noble model" for his novel, a connection which he trusted "the candid and learned reader" would be able to see on his own. It is clear that *Amelia* is patterned after the *Aeneid* in a much more intricate and ambitious way than *Tom Jones* and *Joseph Andrews* can be said to be modeled on the *Odyssey*, to which both these novels may be broadly referred as comic epics of the arduous voyage home. Fielding in fact takes some pains to remind us of the presence of Virgil's epic within *Amelia:* his novel is amply sprinkled with quotations from the Latin and Greek poets, often untranslated, and Virgil, apparently the favorite poet of the learned Mrs. Bennet, is the most frequently quoted or alluded to. George Sherburn first made the observation that *Amelia* includes some parallels to the *Aeneid* of veritably Joycean ingenuity. Thus, in the opening section, Booth is cast into Newgate by chance just as Aeneas at the beginning of Virgil's poem is tossed by fate into Dido's palace. After recounting in prison to Miss Matthews—in the manner of Aeneas to Dido—all that has befallen him in the past seven years, Booth spends a week of bittersweet adulterous pleasure with her in her cell, just as Dido and Aeneas consummate their passion in a Carthaginian cave and pass a brief winter of furtive love together. Sherburn is cautious and tactful in suggesting an anticipation in *Amelia* of the technique Joyce would later make famous; two more recent critics have trampled tact and caution underfoot in running to ground all conceivable parallels to Virgil in Fielding's novel.[2] I tend to doubt whether Fielding actually attempted to sustain the elaborateness of the connection between Booth's story and Aeneas' after the first three books. In any case, the interesting critical question here is not the deciphering of a Virgilian code in Fielding's novel but the problem of why he chose to use an epic model at all in this way, and why the *Aeneid* in particular.

Although Fielding's adaptation of the classic epic is by no means so ambitious as Joyce's, his invention of the technique is a response to an aesthetic challenge which he envisages basically in the same way as Joyce. The novel has often been described, with more portentousness than precision, as the epic of modern life, or of bourgeois society, though it is clear that in any responsible use of the term epic this is simply not true for most novels. The juxtaposition of novel and epic, however, does point toward a fundamental difficulty for the novel as a genre. The subject of the novel, by and large, is banality itself, and so the task that confronts the novelist is to redeem banality through art. How does a writer take that which is so familiar as to be cliché, which reeks of the sordid tedium and triviality of everyday life, and by representing it in art stir the imagination and speak to the condition of many men for all time? One rather special strategy for coping with this difficulty has been the serious parody of traditional myth. Joyce gives larger significance to his down-at-the-heels advertising agent whose life is a patchwork of tawdry daydreams and pathetic frustrations by inviting us to see him as a modern Ulysses, a resilient, resourceful wanderer in search of a son, an exile looking for home. Similarly, Fielding tries to make the muddled failures of a half-pay captain, cheating on his wife and running into debt through weakness and naiveté, seem more important by suggesting analogies between the moral role Booth must play and that of Virgil's Aeneas.

This difficulty with which the novelist, in contrast to the epic poet, is faced might also be stated in terms of the relationship between public and private experience. The sense of magnitude communicated by the epic derives in part from the fact that the epic generally deals with significant collective events, and its heroes, however sharply individual, are collective heroes: the fate of nations, and cultures, hangs upon the delicate and terrible balance of the epic hero's sword, and that is surely one reason why we feel that something vastly important is transpiring through the action of the epic. The characteristic subjects of the novel, on the other hand, have no wider public significance than those depressingly repetitious notations in the back pages of a daily newspaper—the bankruptcy of a respectable businessman, a wedding between a local clergyman and a genteel young lady, the suicide of a provincial doctor's wife. The greatest novelists have generally found ways of using such familiar, private events as seismographs which are capable of registering the most subtle tremors running through the whole social structure and the most critical pressures exerted by the historical moment. An early and striking example of this kind of achievement is the fiction of Jane Austen: her world, which consists of daughters of the landed gentry looking for suitable husbands, is notoriously circumscribed, but her perception of the definition of character and values by social forces is so fine that the little world beautifully catches the significant reverberations of the larger world to which it belongs.

It is clear that Fielding did not possess the kind of delicate apparatus of observation that could enable him to present a subtle interplay of social forces in fictional relationships. Richardson perhaps comes closer to it, though it is not really an excellence one finds in eighteenth-century novelists, whether in England or in France. Fielding's characters, on the whole, are either bizarrely, and delightfully, idiosyncratic, or broadly representative, with only occasional glimpses of the kind of character whose closely observed individuality reveals the social matrix of individual experience. For this reason, a panoramic structure, instead of a tight involvement of personalities at close quarters, is entirely appropriate for his two comic novels. In *Amelia*, however, he sought to make the concerns of the novel at once more private and more public than they had been in either *Tom Jones* or *Joseph Andrews*, and this is finally, I think, the reason for his introducing the *Aeneid* into the story of the domestic difficulties of one William Booth. In the very first sentence of his Dedication, Fielding announces that it is his purpose "to expose some of the most glaring evils, as well public as private, which at present infest this country," and one of the major problems of his novel is the technical means of relating public to private experience. The general allusion to the *Aeneid* reflects Fielding's desire to establish this connection, though it does not really solve his artistic difficulties for him.

Fielding's awareness of the special challenge of *Amelia*, and the special relevance of the epic to that challenge, is nicely expressed in the flat declaration with which he begins the novel: "The various accidents which befell a very worthy couple after their uniting in the state of matrimony will be the subject of the following history." Fielding, as always, is highly conscious of his role as pioneer: with the partial and uncomfortably didactic exception of the continuation of *Pamela*, no novel as yet had attempted to deal with what happens to two people *after* they unite in the state of matrimony, when, in place of the adventures or tensions of courtship, they must bear the heavy and multifarious responsibilities of making a life together. The first sentence of *Amelia* is also the *arma virumque*, the epic proposition of the novel, as George Sherburn observes in his comment on Virgilian allusions. The vicissitudes of this particular young couple are announced at the outset as a subject of the broadest relevance and the gravest moral dignity; and so the narrator immediately goes on to implicate the history of the Booths in the activity of Fortune, just as Aeneas in the first lines of Virgil's poem is seen driven from the shores of Troy by a grand and inexorable *fatum*. Fortune is of course also the subject of much teasing banter by the ostentatiously manipulative narrator of *Tom Jones*, but in *Amelia*, from the very beginning, it is instead seriously discussed, as an idea that shapes men's lives, and part of the philosophical argument of the novel is to refute the pagan concept of Fortune through the action and dialogue.

Amelia is Fielding's one extended attempt to create that

figure with which so many Renaissance writers struggled un-successfully—the Christian hero. Tom Jones is not, in any clearly indispensable way, Christian in such heroism as he possesses, and Parson Adams is not really a hero, but Booth is a man of heroic qualities, compromised by bad judgment and a dangerous malleability, who must learn as a husband and father to live a Christian life in a pagan world. In this central respect, the *Aeneid* is most relevant as a model, for it is the great epic of duty, the very epic, in fact, sometimes thought of by Christian tradition itself as a sort of proto-Christian poem. Both Aeneas and Booth are soldiers by calling, men who have to perform duties, submit to a rigorous disci-pline; and the quality of *pietas*—reverent loyalty, implicit obedience to the gods as they work out their purpose in human lives—associated with Aeneas involves a series of painful re-nunciations which enable him to become a perfect instrument for the divine plan in history. Fielding, to be sure, is not concerned in his novel with the larger reaches of history, but he does want to draw attention to the effect of provi-dential design in individual lives, and his hero, whom we first see mouthing arrant deism and then in dalliance with a mod-ern-day Dido, must learn to renounce his "un-Roman" weakness of conviction—his belief in an insuperable Ruling Passion which provides him an excuse for moral flaccidity—in order to assume the responsibilities of his destiny as the worthy mate of the true Christian wife, Amelia. Booth's role as Chris-tian soldier, incidentally, explains the attention given in the novel to the polemic against dueling—a pagan conception of honor, or love and honor, must be exorcised before an authen-tically Christian hero can come into being.

This identification between a pristine Roman society and pristine Christianity is characteristically Augustan. As in the weightiest of Augustan satire—notably, Swift and the later Pope—the atmosphere of the novel is filled with darkening shadows, is suffused with a sense that the true Roman, or

Christian, values have slipped away in a process of disastrous cultural and moral decline. The point is made explicit in an exchange between Dr. Harrison and the lord whose aid he futilely attempts to enlist to get Booth a commission:

"Indeed, doctor," cries the lord, "all these notions are obsolete and long since exploded. To apply maxims of government drawn from the Greek and Roman histories to this nation is absurd and impossible. But, if you will have Roman examples, fetch them from those times of the republic that were most like our own. Do you not know, doctor, that this is as corrupt a nation as ever existed under the sun? And would you think of governing such a people by the strict principles of honesty and morality?"

"If it be so corrupt," said the doctor, "I think it is high time to amend it: or else it is easy to foresee that Roman and British liberty will have the same fate; for corruption in the body politic as naturally tends to dissolution as in the natural body." (XI, 2)

Rome after the period of high achievement of the empire is clearly associated in the novel with England after the abandonment of the moral imperatives of Christianity. As Dr. Harrison observes elsewhere (IX, 5), in a phrase reminiscent of *Joseph Andrews*, "I no more esteem this nation to be . . . a Christian society . . . than I do any part of Turkey." But the treatment of the Christian–pagan opposition is qualitatively different in the two novels. In *Joseph Andrews*, the Christianity of the protagonists is a given thing, unaffected— indeed, unalterable—by experience. In *Amelia* Fielding attempts to show how an unchristian society prevents a man from being a Christian, and how he may manage to behave as a Christian nevertheless. To put this difference in terms of a moral psychology, Fielding in the earlier novels had presented human nature in what might almost be thought of as a Manichean split, humanity congenitally divided into children of light and children of darkness, men of Good Heart and Mean Spirit, with, however, some interesting cases in between. In *Amelia,* on the other hand, the old dichotomy of good and bad nature is partly replaced by another one of human nature and society. Even a scheming lecher like Colonel James, Dr. Harrison suggests in the passage just quoted, could have been a good man had he lived in a Christian society. "Bad education," Harrison argues, "bad habits, and bad customs, debauch our nature, and drive it headlong . . . into vice. The governors of the world, and I am afraid the priesthood, are answerable for the badness of it."

Amelia, then, is among other things an embryonic novel of social protest. In the earlier novels, corruption is a predictable consequence of human nature which tends to center in the city, and which is known, condemned, and at last avoided, more or less, by a prudent retreat to the country. One can guess that Fielding's deep involvement in his work as police magistrate had led him, by the time he wrote *Amelia,* to a new concern for the ways in which corruption was endemic to a particular social, political, and legal system. It is the cold, unyielding, arbitrary force of the corrupt system that one feels in *Amelia* at many of the novel's most persuasive moments. Thus the action begins with the nocturnal arraignment of Booth by Justice Thrasher, a figure who in his rapacious greed, savage arbitrariness, and arrogant ignorance of the law, makes the obtuse justices of the peace in *Joseph Andrews* and *Tom Jones* look like paragons of judiciary wisdom and rectitude. Shortly after Booth is brought into Newgate, the narrator devotes an entire chapter (I, 4) to a darkly satiric panorama of victims of the law: in a manner and mood that look forward to the mature Dickens, we see how the most innocent individuals are ruthlessly crushed by an insane system while the worst scoundrels continue to commit their crimes with impunity.

The terrible wrongness of the system is most painfully apparent in the predicament of Booth. The power to arrest debtors is used against him by the rich would-be seducers of his wife simply to clear him out of the conjugal bed. No matter how many avenues of influence he explores, his efforts to obtain a commission in the army are hopeless; and while he, an experienced officer of proved valor, starves with his family on half-pay, footmen and noblemen's pimps are appointed to positions of command, and spoiled boys, with the first fuzz of puberty on their cheeks, are advanced to captaincies. It is no wonder that the crowd breaking into the bailiff's house at the end of the novel is compared to the ocean inundating the land when the dikes give way in Holland: although Fielding the conservative would have been shocked at any drawing of revolutionary inferences from his work, we at times get a sense in the novel of a system so utterly corrupt that nothing will do for it but to sweep it away in a great cataclysm.

Fielding had sought to expose vice in his earlier novels but he had never before attempted actually to indict the social system. He came closest to it in *Jonathan Wild,* but his strategy of attack there was that of formal satire, through a generalizing rhetorical design and highly schematized narrative pattern. In *Amelia,* on the other hand, he tries to carry out the indictment through novelistic means, showing how the lives of particularized, credible individuals are entangled in the insidious mesh of a pervasively venal social order. His basic problem, then, in his last work of fiction is how to go about doing something new for him and, really, new for the novel as a genre. The procedures he developed in his two previous novels could help him in some ways to deal with his problem, but they could also lead him astray, since much of his technique of comic fiction was wholly inappropriate for a novel more seriously engaged in exposing the institutionalized malfunctions of contemporary life.

The use of formal theme, elaborated through reiteration and variation, which we saw in the comic novels, does lend a strength of assertion and a breadth of social perspective to the moral argument of *Amelia*. The central theme of marriage is firmly announced in the first of the two epigraphs, and the entire novel can be seen as a panorama of unions, marital and extramarital, good and bad, though mostly the latter. Marriage is conceived as the basic institution of both private life and Christian society—making a good home takes on the kind of importance in this novel that the founding of the empire is given in Virgil's poem—so that the prevalent neglect, violation, and loveless manipulation of marriage become measures of the failure of Christian values in society at large.

The first extended narrative in the novel is concerned with an illicit union, Miss Matthews' story of her ill-considered liaison with the unscrupulous Hebbers. This is followed by Booth's account of his true love match with Amelia, which ironically, ends up being the prelude to his week-long adulterous connection with Miss Matthews. After Booth is freed from prison, we have an opportunity to see the mutual loyalty and affection of his marriage with Amelia, while over against the Booths are set the Jameses, a Fashionable Couple out of the pages of Restoration comedy, each spouse heartily despising the other and at least one of them always on the lookout for amorous intrigues. Colonel James's description of a tolerable wife rings with echoes of the sundry Dorimants and Rhodophils and Fainalls of the Restoration stage, those jaded hedonistic spokesmen of a thoroughly unchristian society: "With the spirit of a tigress I would have her be a prude, a scold, a scholar, a critic, a wit, a politician, and a jacobite; and then, perhaps, eternal opposition would keep up our spirits; and, wishing one another daily at the devil, we should make a shift to drag on a damnable state of life, without much spleen or vapors" (V, 9). The poetic justice administered to Colonel James at the end of the novel is nicely adjusted to his contemptuous abuse of the married state: divorced at last from his wife, he takes Miss Matthews into keeping and comes to dote on her, while she, grown fat and ugly, uses him ruthlessly as a kind of servile retainer.

Another military couple, the Trents, who appear late in the novel, are a more tawdry, visibly degraded version of the Jameses. Their initial passion for each other has quickly cooled, and Trent then establishes himself in the world by selling his entirely amenable wife to the Noble Lord and afterward becoming chief procurer for that lecherous gentleman. In contrast to these corrupt unions, the first and second marriages of Mrs. Bennet are models of faithful affection, though more imperfect than the marriage of Amelia and Booth: the happiness of her first union is poisoned by her own weakness in succumbing to the scheming peer, and her subsequent marriage with Atkinson is somewhat flawed by the wife's sense of intellectual superiority to the husband. Finally, hovering above all these married figures as the spirit of anti-matrimony in the novel is the shadowy presence of the Noble Lord. A sinister descendant of the ubiquitous Horners of Restoration comedy, his main object in life is seducing virtuous wives, and his notion of a relationship with a woman is to use her body for a night, or at best for a week or two.

It should be noted that in all this Fielding is moving toward a new kind of integration of narrative and thematic materials, a first anticipation of the masterful interlocking of separate lives through shared situation that gives *Middlemarch* such remarkable structural coherence. The accounts of the respective unions of Miss Matthews and Hebbers, of the Booths, the Jameses, the Bennets, the Trents, are all narrative regressions, but they all relate to the principal thematic concern of the novel more directly than the interpolated tales of *Joseph Andrews* and *Tom Jones,* and they are connected with each other bodily, as it were, not just thematically. The body that does most of the connecting is the Noble Lord's: Fielding's attempt to make him work as a figure at once peripheral and absolutely central to the major action is an interesting, though not altogether successful, technical experiment.

The key to the anomalous status of this promiscuous peer

is, I think, his peculiar anonymity. We normally expect a novelist to give individual names to his personages because we look in the novel not for a summary or abstraction of experience but for a persuasive re-creation of the world as we know it, in all its stubborn and prickly particularity. That is why *Moll Flanders,* with its cast of nameless figures whose identity is exhausted in the role they play vis à vis Moll, is only rudimentarily a novel. Some critics have argued that the distinctive approach of the novel to fictional character is reflected in its choice of names that could have been lifted —as in fact they sometimes are—straight out of the city directory. This is partly true and partly misleading. Fielding's own practice in *Joseph Andrews* and *Tom Jones* is to assign obviously symbolic names to many of his characters, and a great many novelists, from Dickens and Dostoevski to Joyce and Nabokov, have adopted the same method, though usually with a greater attempt at camouflage. Fielding uses symbolic names in his first two novels in order to hold his characters at a comic distance, as elements of a conscious artifice, and because each of the characters is conceived as a particular embodiment of some general moral (or social) role, posture, value. In *Amelia,* on the other hand, the writer exhibits a new empiric openness in imagining his characters, and so all of them, with the exception of Justice Thrasher and Bailiff Bondum, who are the subjects of incidental satirical vignettes, are given quite neutral, realistic names—Booth, Matthews, James, Robinson, Harrison, Trent, Ellison, and so forth. The moral identity of these characters is, to begin with, uncertain, and they will be whatever we can make of them by closely following their words and deeds.

The Noble Lord, however, is left without a name, for Fielding means him to be a vague and generalized presence, almost always kept offstage, the ubiquitous spirit of corruption of a degenerate aristocracy, manipulating the lives of the weak through a chain of underlings and procurers, ready to carry out that nasty little piece of business wherever an innocent woman in England leaves herself vulnerable. The trouble is that a figure so conceived scarcely belongs in the fictional world of this novel. For the general tendency of *Amelia,* however intermittently pursued, is toward a more psychologically individual realization of character, while the Noble Lord is a psychological vacuity of a sort one scarcely finds in either *Joseph Andrews* or *Tom Jones.* He owes something, perhaps, to the satirically generalized figures of *Jonathan Wild,* the schematically designed personages of a mode of fiction alien to that of *Amelia.* Where we might hope for a representative individual who could dramatize the complexities of an obsessional concern with the sexual exploitation of innocence, we get instead a mysterious absence which looks at times almost comical, and that is surely a serious weakness in the novel.

In any case, the Noble Lord serves as the exemplar of that way of life in which adultery is the chief activity, and adultery itself is a kind of paradigm of all that is wrong in a society where Christian values have been discarded. "It includes in it," Dr. Harrison writes of adultery in the letter to Colonel James which is the object of such ridicule at the masquerade, "almost every injury and every mischief which one man can do to, or can bring upon, another" (X, 2). Adultery, that is to say, is the perfect expression of a ruthlessly egoistic hedonism, a cynically exploitative, utterly disengaged relationship to humanity which makes a man willing to inflict all kinds of suffering on others for the sake of his own momentary gratification. In *Tom Jones* all the sexual liaisons, with the single exception of Mrs. Fitzgerald's, are merely promiscuous, not adulterous, for what "prudence" mainly implies in that novel is an individual's moral responsibilities to himself. In *Amelia,* on the other hand, Fielding is more deeply concerned with the individual's responsibilities to others and to society, and with society's responsibilities to the individual, and so he makes almost all the illicit unions in the novel adulterous. Adultery, it is clear, is a kind of sexual indulgence that often impinges painfully on the lives of others, on the very institution of the family; and a general commitment to the relentless pursuit of adulterous pleasures serves as an apt symbol for a morally irresponsible social system. Fielding chose his subject, then, with a sound sense of strategic appropriateness, but because he had no previous experience or direct models in writing a novel of social indictment, he tends to waver in his treatment of the subject between novelistic and unfortunately homiletic methods.

On the novelistic side, he takes up the familiar theme of mask and disguise from *Tom Jones* and makes it reverberate with a new amplitude through the world of *Amelia*, where a whole society is dedicated to keeping up false appearances and using them to gain illegitimate ends. At the very beginning of the action (I, 2), we are told of Justice Thrasher, the symbolic representative of a corrupt system, that he had "too great an honor for Truth to suspect that she ever appeared in sordid apparel." Though this reverence for the outward forms of wealth—"virtue" construed as power—is shared by many characters in both *Joseph Andrews* and *Tom Jones,* it immediately has graver implications here because Thrasher's vital professional responsibility is to discriminate truth from falsehood, and because he also has the power, as we see at once, to act swiftly and arbitrarily on his venal impulses. The sundry seducers of innocence in the novel are all skilled in putting on virtuous appearances: Dr. Harrison is a little staggered that Colonel James could hide such villainy "under the appearance of so much virtue" (IX, 5), and the narrator comments to the same effect on "that noble art" which enables the colonel to look delighted at an unexpected, and dismaying, meeting with Amelia's husband: "By this [art], men are enabled to dress out their countenances as much at their own pleasure as they do their bodies, and to put on friendship with as much ease as they can a laced coat" (IX, 2). In the light of such observations, we can see why the action of the novel begins on April Fool's Day, a pointedly appropriate juncture at which to introduce us to a world of deceivers and contrived illusions.

It is almost inevitable that the central rite of such a society should be the masquerade. Fielding here alludes to literary tradition as well as to social practice: the significance of the masquerade in *Amelia* looks back to the moral meaning of the masquerade in Restoration comedy—most appositely, in Dryden's *Marriage à la Mode*—where assuming the mask is an invitation to saturnalian release, a means not merely of deception but of escape from the responsibilities of personality. At the masquerade, at least as it appears in Restoration literature and as it is used in this novel, hungry sexual egos go stalking after ready partners, everyone hiding behind a glittering facade that protects him from involvement, allows him to forget in a relationship between masks and bodies the commitments of relationships between persons, the limitations and obligations imposed by family and society in ordinary maskless life. It is therefore symbolically right that the Noble Lord should make his conquest of Mrs. Bennet's virtue upon returning with her from a masquerade, and that he should attempt to do the same favor for Amelia by inviting her to another masked ball. The spectacle of a crowd of insolent young rakes at the masquerade making a mockery of Dr. Harrison's sermon-letter on adultery nicely dramatizes the central opposition of the novel—a true Christianity preached with desperate insistence to an unheeding pagan world of brazen hearts and masked faces.

One of Fielding's most significant innovations in *Amelia*, though he fails to carry it out consistently, is his translation of this sense of a masked humanity into a new method of characterization. The pervasive feeling in *Tom Jones* that Nature will eventually peep out from even the most elaborate disguise is attenuated in *Amelia*: a principal reason for the drastic curtailment of authorial intervention in the latter novel is that the narrator does not want to suggest he holds Nature, or that part of it which relates to his personages, within the secure round of his cunningly cupped hands, to be revealed when he sees fit. John Coolidge has aptly described the new mode of presenting character which begins to emerge in *Amelia:* "People come into the story in the same way that people come into our lives . . . Our knowledge of a person's character is always provisory, pending further discovery. A new word or act may bring a new revelation, causing a shift in our interpretation and evaluation of a person's character." [3] This is, perhaps, more a description of the unrealized paradigm toward which Fielding was moving than of his actual practice throughout the novel, for the characterization, even in the more interesting of the major personages, seems to wobble between the old "high priori way" of the two comic novels and the new method of progressive discovery.

Although the new technique is applied unevenly, it does implicate the reader directly in the experience of a world where any smiling face may turn out to be a mask, where, indeed, the face behind the mask may sometimes prove to be but another mask. Though the writer seems to settle in the end for a simple view of his own characters, his method of presentation makes us alive to the essential trickiness— the elusiveness as well as the duplicity—of human nature. Thus Colonel James at first really seems to be the most generous and loyal of friends, but we gradually learn that the gold he showers on Booth is intended to buy his way to Amelia's bed. Nevertheless, there is a teasing uncertainty in James's transition from stalwart friend to dastardly villain. On the evidence of the later chapters, I would assume that Fielding finally conceived him as he had conceived Blifil—a thorough scoundrel to be unmasked in the end. The initial impression, however, of James as a sincere benefactor is strong enough not to be easily dissipated. Perhaps Fielding meant us to conclude that the Colonel's initial generosity to Booth was solely the result of his designs on Amelia, but that is not altogether clear: the inferential method of presenting character leaves us room to wonder whether a man may not, after all, be an admirable, honestly disinterested friend, until he takes too close a look at the fair figure of his friend's wife and so converts his friendship into a contemptible instrumentality. As with Miss Matthews, Mrs. Atkinson, Mrs. Ellison, even Mrs. James, the characterization of the colonel would appear to point toward complexities and ambiguities which Fielding himself was not quite ready to confront or follow out.[4]

Fielding's growing concern, then, with the opacities of human nature and with the threatening moral murkiness of contemporary society is in some ways effectively translated into the method of elaborating theme and presenting character. As for the authorial voice of *Amelia*, because its more shrilly hortatory tones are likely to linger uncomfortably in the ear of the imagination, it needs to be stressed that Fielding also succeeds in working out in some passages of the novel a new, trenchant kind of irony, skillfully adjusted to the new earnestness of moral and social criticism. The narrator stays half-hidden in the wings much of the time, but his occasional appearances before the proscenium arch, in a manner quite different from that of *Tom Jones*, are revealing. At the end of a chapter, for example, in which we see one of the first great instances of the munificence of Colonel James to Booth, the narrator steps forward, ostensibly to point the moral:

Here, reader, give me leave to stop a minute, to lament that so few are to be found of this benign disposition; that, while wantonness, vanity, avarice, and ambition are every day rioting and triumphing in the follies and weakness, the ruin and desolation of mankind, scarce one man in a thousand is capable of tasting the happiness of others. Nay, give me leave to wonder that pride, which is constantly struggling, and often imposing on itself, to gain some little pre-eminence,

should seldom hint to us the only certain as well as laudable way of
setting ourselves above another man, and that is, by becoming his
benefactor. (IV, 4)

This is shrewd irony, but to rather a different purpose than
that of the comic novels. The plea for altruism and the condemnation of a viciously selfish society in the first sentence
are quite serious, yet they also provide a false lead to draw
us into the ironic trap of the sentence that follows. As we
begin to nod in complacent assent—or boredom—to the proper
moral cadences of the sermonic narrator, he quickly concedes
that overweening pride is the universal spring of action, and,
contrary to all Christian doctrine on charity, he invites us to
give unto others—so that we may affirm our own towering superiority to them. There is no certain indication that this egotistic motive is meant to apply to the beneficence of Colonel
James, of whom we were told just a moment earlier that
"generous he really was to the highest degree," but I think
the ambiguity is intentional. We have not yet been given
any hint of the colonel's interest in Amelia: when we eventually learn of that, the serious and ironic defense of generosity
here is compounded by a graver doubt, a further possibility
of irony.

In *Tom Jones,* the doubleness of the irony is an invitation
to suspend judgment, or delicately balance contradictory claims,
to step back from humanity and survey it in the round, in all the
perplexities and piquant or pathetic self-delusions of its motives.
The strategies of *Amelia,* on the other hand, generally lead us
toward a closer involvement in the moral predicaments of the
novel, and, to a lesser degree, in the lives of the characters. The
irony in the passage we have been considering is contrived to
snap shut on the reader at the end, to produce not bemused
contemplation but an unsettling confrontation, forcing us to face
up to the terribly compromised nature of all men's motives, our
own included.

The presence of this kind of authorial irony in *Amelia* suggests that it would have been possible for Fielding to have retained a successfully subdued version of his self-conscious narrator while making his readers confront the moral action with a new kind of troubled personal involvement. His desire, however, to conduct an urgent moral argument through his novel leads him in many instances to adopt what I have referred to as homiletic procedures. In the prefatory sections of his two comic novels, he had spoken about using fiction as a means of offering to the reader a variety of moral exempla, but fortunately he never carried out that promise with the singleness of purpose we encounter at some points in *Amelia*. Thus, in IV, 3, in the first of a series of moral tableaux of domestic life, Booth, ridden with debts and the guilty consciousness of his recent adultery, is given new testimony of Amelia's loving confidence in him, even amidst the hardships of poverty, and he prostrates himself at her feet. At this juncture, the narrator raises his didactic pointer to the two posed figures, and comments: "Such is ever the fortitude of perfect innocence, and such the depression of guilt in minds not utterly abandoned." One does not want to begrudge Amelia her virtue, but the explicit moralizing is uncomfortably insistent, and, throughout the novel, the contrast between husband and wife is often heavily overdrawn.

Action and dialogue as well as authorial comment are palpably contrived so that this contrast will stand out. We see Amelia depriving herself and her young ones of food, pawning her only valuable possessions, while Booth squanders fifty pounds at a time over the card table. When Booth, visited by Amelia at the bailiff's after his second arrest for debt, learns that she all along has known of—and forgiven—his affair with Miss Matthews, the narrator's underscoring of the all-too-obvious moral contrast is almost embarrassing: "Amelia never shined forth to Booth in so amicable and great a light; nor did his own unworthiness ever appear to him so mean and contemptible as at this instant" (XII, 2).

To view the novel gastronomically, there are lumps of undigested didactic matter in *Amelia* that sometimes block the flow of fictional reality. It would seem that Fielding, anxious to show the cogency of a practical ethical doctrine, did not know quite how to get it all into novelistic terms. So it is that he incorporates into the novel formal debates on religious and philosophical questions, which are connected to the surrounding narrative solely by the ideas discussed. At the bailiff's, Booth encounters a gentleman (VIII, 10) who is unnamed, uncharacterized, unrelated to the main action, whose only purpose is to engage Booth in a dialogue on stoic fortitude in adversity and the power of the Ruling Passion. The two debates (IX, 8 and 10) between Dr. Harrison and the young clergyman—again, symptomatically, a character without a name—are static interruptions of the novel's progress, with none of the cunning counterpoint of interpolation and main narrative that one finds in *Joseph Andrews* and *Tom Jones*. While the tribulations of Amelia and Booth must patiently wait their turn for our attention, the good doctor and the young clergyman conduct a learned argument, matching quotations and the commentators thereon, about the proper Christian attitude toward one's enemies and the role of a clergyman in a society devoid of Christian values. The revelation at the end of the second debate that the young man's father has been merely feigning agreement with the doctor, out of worldly interest, is an attempt to relate satirically these disquisitions on moral theory to the novel's dramatized world of self-seeking hypocrisy. Both chapters, however, remain heavily expository, with only perfunctory attempts to sustain the novelistic life of realized personalities responding to one another.

Similarly, even in the less theoretical exchanges between the principal characters, speech is sometimes formalized and generalized in an unnatural way to point a moral. Booth is not content to tell his story to Miss Matthews but must call attention to what his story teaches: "In this dreadful situation we were taught that no human condition should inspire men with absolute despair" (III, 4); and Amelia at times sounds more like a moral essayist than a wife comforting her husband in distress: "How many thousands abound in affluence whose fortunes are much lower than ours! for it is not from nature, but from education and habit, that our wants are chiefly derived" (IV, 3).

A small but most significant symptom of this whole didactic weakness in *Amelia* is the fact that at one point (IX, 1) the narrator turns to a particular segment of his audience, "my young readers," before beginning a homiletic excursus. In *Tom Jones*, we recall, the assumed reader was an intelligent man of the world with whom the narrator could share sly hints, innuendos, cunning ironies, tempered judgments of moral acts. The reader at this point in *Amelia*, however, begins to look suspiciously like that bloodless figure with a mind as innocent and unsubstantial as a lily petal, the Young Person of Victorian literature, for whom so much bland and emptily self-righteous stuff was written. It is such "young readers" who are the proper subject for moral instruction uncomplicated by any ironic awareness, as in the sermon in two paragraphs here on the unguessed perils of temptation in woman's beauty. Fortunately, such passages are not altogether typical: Fielding's sense of audience, so essential to the achievement of *Joseph Andrews* and *Tom Jones,* is simply uneven in this novel. At some points, he reflects a subtle consciousness of a sophisticated audience with serious moral concerns; sometimes, as here, he credits his readers with too little experience and sometimes, as we shall see, with too much.

The didacticism of *Amelia*, which results in exhortations to the reader from both narrator and personages, also has a damaging effect on some of the characterization, particularly in the two exemplary figures of the novel, Dr. Harrison and Amelia. The dialectic irony which qualified the virtuous characters in the two comic novels is nowhere in evidence here; Fielding seems afraid to do anything that might undermine or mitigate the exemplariness of his models of virtue. In the case of Dr. Harrison, the gap between the author's own promise and performance is instructive. Although we are told (IX, 5) that "the doctor was one of the best companions in the world, and a vein of cheerfulness, good humor, and pleasantry, ran through his conversation, with which it was impossible to resist being pleased," there are scarcely two attempts in the whole novel to show us Harrison's good-humored jocularity, and one is hard put to think of a character in fiction whose supposed charm is easier to resist. This is especially remarkable because Fielding, of all eighteenth-century novelists, surely had the ability to create an engagingly witty character; but he apparently was unwilling to relent for a moment from reminding us of Dr. Harrison's grave role as Christian censor and image of the Good Pastor.

Amelia gives a little more promise of assuming real life as a character, in her frankly feminine awareness of her own attractiveness, and, occasionally, in her response to her husband, as, for example, when she is refreshingly resentful—of course within the proper limits of a virtuous wife's submission—to her husband's unexplained command that she not accept the ticket to the masquerade (IV, 6). More often, though, we see her frozen in the conventional poses of virtuous womanhood, a sort of modern version of the Worthy Wife of Proverbs XXXI —embracing her innocent young ones, waiting loyally long into the night for the return of her wayward husband, pleading before the great to save him from destruction. "Art thou really human," Booth exclaims in one of his fits of adulation, "or art thou rather an angel in human form?" (X, 6), and the reader may be tempted to answer the rhetorical question with an irony that Fielding never intended.

The conception of both the heroine and the central situation of *Amelia* is, finally, parabolic, and unlike the biblical symbolism in *Joseph Andrews* or the submerged hint of allegory in *Tom Jones* (Tom in search of Wisdom, Sophia, whose handmaiden is Honour), the parable is not entirely assimilated to the novel form. Dr. Harrison at one point refers to Amelia in terms which transparently reveal the kind of symbolic function she is meant to serve: "She hath a true Christian disposition. I may call her an Israelite indeed, in whom there is no guile" (IX, 8). His words echo those addressed by Jesus to Nathanael in John 1.47, and the allusion to John suggests an interesting imaginative affinity, for of all the gospels, John is the one that consistently converts physical facts into spiritual symbols, and the one in which the central figure of Jesus is most transcendently divine, least sympathetically human. If Fielding had attempted before to present an Israelite indeed, in whom there was no guile, in the person of Abraham Adams, he also had a novelist's keen awareness that it can be a grotesque liability to be without guile in an unredeemed world of cheats and hypocrites. His spiritual gravity as parabolist, however, leads him to suppress such awareness in the characterization of Amelia.

John iconically translates the flesh-and-blood Jesus into the Lamb of God, and Amelia, the true Christian, the sacrificial wife, the vulnerable innocent, is also a lamb of sorts. Why, the narrator asks rhetorically, should a poor wretch like Booth, imprisoned through the machinations of Colonel James, be the object of the colonel's envy? "Because this wretch was possessed of the affections of a poor little lamb, which all the vast flocks that were within the power and the reach of the colonel could not prevent that glutton's longing for" (VIII, 8). The allusion, of course, is to the parable of the poor man's lamb used by Nathan the prophet in his condemnation of David, who arranged the death of Bathsheba's husband so that he could have her for himself (II Samuel 12). Actually, there are indications in the biblical story that Bathsheba was not quite so innocent or helpless as the lamb of Nathan's parable: she might have made a more interesting heroine for a novel than Amelia, who too often is merely a symbolic figure in a tale told to prod conscience, not a credible personality whose story can open the imagination to the multifarious and nuanced possibilities of humanity in a particular society.

There is, moreover, an element of contradiction or at least tension between the conception of the novel as moral parable and the novelist's aims of social criticism. Although Fielding is obviously aware in *Amelia* that many of the institutions of society are not what they should be, he ultimately sees the pervasive corruption which is his subject as a derivative of the moral life of individuals. The vagueness of this viewpoint is apparent in an exchange between Booth and Amelia at the very end of Book X. "Compassion," Booth argues, is "the fellow-feeling only of men of the same rank and degree of life for one another, on account of the evils to which they themselves are liable." Booth would appear to be echoing the Mandevillian doctrine of self-love as the universal motive, though his words raise a question—which Fielding, with his fundamentally conservative imagination, never confronts—as to whether some other kind of social order might be possible, where men would not be so utterly alienated from each other by rank and degree. Amelia, in any case, responds to her husband's account of the inhumanity of society with a well-meaning moralism, clearly speaking for Fielding as she repeats the maxim of Terence's which she has heard from Dr. Harrison: *"I am a man myself, and my heart is interested in whatever can befall the rest of mankind.* That is the sentiment of a good man, and whoever thinks otherwise is a bad one." It is worth noting that Dr. Harrison's paraphrase of the Latin introduces one distinctly un-Roman notion—the interested heart. The world would be better, Amelia suggests, if every man would just have a Good Heart, if people would be good and not bad. Because Fielding tends to slip into this kind of pious moral generality, he never fully engages the social aspects of his subject: there is a hiatus between the private and public concerns which were announced in the first sentence of the Dedication as the subject of the novel.

That hiatus is probably most conspicuous in the denouement. The comic happy ending, in which interlopers are
banished, lovers harmoniously united, and undreamt of estates
made to tumble down out of heaven, is entirely appropriate
in *Joseph Andrews* and *Tom Jones,* for both those novels are
consciously selective artifices which implicitly assure us, by
the providential presence of the artificer, that all things rightful
will be finally bestowed upon all the right people. Fielding's
attitude, moreover, toward the conventional ending is more
slyly ironic than most readers give him credit for: he surely
means to tip us the wink, one last time, when at the end of
Tom Jones he hastily marries off his paragon of crude female
lust, Molly Seagrim, to the timorous Partridge, and the ener-
getically sensual Mrs. Waters to that most spineless of clergy-
men, Parson Supple. In *Amelia,* on the other hand, Fielding
uses the happy ending as his Victorian imitators did and as
hostile critics have imagined he did in *Tom Jones*—to clap
together some conventional happiness for his protagonists
which does not necessarily follow from the logic of the novel
itself. Plots constructed, or at least concluded, in this way
are, to borrow Ford Madox Ford's vehement phrase, "dangers
to the body-politic," for they evade the responsibilities of the
moral issues which the novelist himself has raised.

Booth's conversion, as has often been observed, is hardly
credible because it comes so suddenly, without any psychological preparation: the metamorphosis of Booth the deist into
Booth the good Christian is a final reflection of that tendency
in *Amelia* to moral schematism which we have been considering. More to our present purpose, the miraculous recovery of
Amelia's estate seems like too easy a way out here because
the whole novel has been concerned with the absolute failure
of the social system to recognize merit, and the apparently
irreversible trend of the whole crooked system is to crush all
poor innocents like Booth. Since there is no happy solution to
Booth's predicament within the system, Fielding invokes another schematism, converting Booth's pagan Fortune to Provi-

dence with the hero's own conversion, and so he ends up using Dr. Harrison as a fairy godfather to waft the Booths with a magic wand away from the really hopeless snares and delusions of London to their own true home in the country.

To complete this account of the weaknesses in *Amelia*, one aspect of the novel must be mentioned which is not so much a matter of uncertain artistic purpose as of unfortunate intellectual fashion. The moral view that informs this novel, as we have seen, places the locus of mankind's redemption in men's hearts, the potential goodness of which becomes a first principle of faith, and rather too heavy a load is put upon that frail organ from a novelistic as well as a moral point of view. Fielding alerts us at once, in the third paragraph of the Dedication, to the fact that this novel is directed to a special kind of reader: "The good-natured reader, if his heart should be here affected, will be inclined to pardon many faults for the pleasure he will receive from a tender sensation." Now, the "sagacious reader" of *Tom Jones* was also credited with good nature and expected to be moved by scenes of virtue, but the conjunction here of heart, pleasure, and tender sensation is reaching toward a kind of experience alien to the comic spirit of Fielding's two previous novels. Much eighteenth-century literature, even that which is usually thought of as coolly intellectual, contains an undercurrent of craving for intense and sublime sensation: by the sixties and seventies, the undercurrent had become a mainstream in the literary vogue now generally referred to as the cult of sensibility. Fielding had already given intimations of his interest in effects of sensibility in the pathetic stories of the Andersons and the Millers in *Tom Jones;* now in *Amelia*, sensibility becomes a central concern, and it is one which plainly militates against novel writing.

Surely one reason why so few good English novels were produced in the last decades of the eighteenth century was the predominance in that period of the cult of sensibility. For the novel, after all, begins with a lucid vision of familiar reality, seen in the varied richness of its concrete particulars, while the focus of writers of sensibility blurs into mysterious and limitless penumbras of experience, vaguely apprehended. The novel is founded on a supreme confidence in the power of language to incorporate reality; even kinds of experience which might seem to be beyond the limits of massive verbal reconstruction—daydream, fantasy, hallucination, fragmented memory, contradictory motivation, preconscious desire—become plastic subjects for novelistic manipulation. The cult of sensibility, on the other hand, insists on the primacy of the ineffable: the most desirable end to which a literary vehicle can convey us is to a love (or joy, or pathos) that passeth understanding and the limits of language as well.

Fielding intends a touchingly tender relationship between Booth and Amelia to be the imaginative center of his novel, but because his assumptions about representing the emotions are essentially those of the writers of sensibility, he constantly refuses to realize that relationship novelistically, in psychological or factual details, in particularizing language. The various narrators of *Amelia* repeatedly allude to the ineffability of the experiences they attempt to report—"raptures not to be expressed," "an ecstasy not to be described," and more of the like. "Shall I tell you what I felt at that instant?" Booth asks Miss Matthews as he relates to her a painful leave-taking from Amelia. "I do assure you I am not able. So many tender ideas crowded at once into my mind, that, if I may use the expression, they almost dissolved my heart" (III, 3). The apology for the expression hardly dilutes its stickiness or mitigates its hyperbolic inadequacy. Later on, when the narrator confesses his inability to convey the pathos of Amelia, weeping with her children who have been bereft of their beloved father, he reveals his underlying semantic assumption: "The scene that followed . . . is beyond my power of description; I must beg the readers' hearts to suggest it to themselves" (VIII, 3).

Where, we may wonder, does the heart get such marvelous

knowledge to reach beyond the mystic borders of the inexpressible? Fielding's answer is simple enough: the heart knows by already having been there. Booth makes the point quite clear in concluding his description to Miss Matthews of the pathetic scene in which he parted from Amelia in order to join the expedition to Gibraltar: "This I am convinced of, that no one is capable of tasting such a scene who hath not a heart of tenderness, and perhaps not even then, unless he hath been in the same situation" (III, 2). And when he reports his and Amelia's reunion with the child they left behind in England—a kind of narrative inconvenience who has been complacently forgotten and now is introduced as an afterthought—he invokes the same principle of communication: "The transports we felt on this occasion were really enchanting, nor can any but a fond parent conceive, I am certain, the least idea of them" (III, 11).

Nothing could illustrate more clearly how the assumptions of the cult of sensibility go against the generic grain of the novel. The literature of sensibility generally takes it for granted that emotional responses to the universal human experiences are everywhere the same—that is why it so frequently draws upon stock situations and characters and fixed verbal formulas, the flow of sensibility naturally spilling over into the clichés of sentimentalism. The only significant variation in response to experience will be one of degree, depending upon the fineness of the individual sensorium, how tender the heart. Logically, then, the best way for a writer to convey a particular emotion is to point to a shared experience—you who are a parent must know what I felt—and without the shared experience, he can communicate little, for only the already loving heart can know love. The novel, on the other hand, that most imperialistic of genres, characteristically seeks to extend its domain to all the little nooks and crannies of both society and the mind, whether or not its readers have been there themselves. The novelist of course begins with the common humanity of us all, but what especially fascinates him is the endlessly varied differences by which men are distinguished from one another, and he often uses the power of imaginative language to transform the otherness of others into familiar objects of our own inner space. If we try to imagine Dostoevski writing, "The exquisite mental torture which Raskolnikov felt, only one who has committed murder will understand," or Faulkner explaining that "Only a true lunatic could have any idea of what went on in Benjy's mind at that moment," we can see how far the assumptions of the cult of sensibility lead us from the novelistic representation of individual experience. A good novel, to be sure, does not have to center on the representation of consciousness, but the new emphasis upon emotional experience in *Amelia* calls for a much closer approach to consciousness than Fielding's habits as a writer and his semantic assumptions will allow him to give us.

The cult of sensibility, finally, is a quest for sensation in itself, and since mere sensations are both impersonal and asocial, their cultivation in fiction tends to preclude that convincing representation of individual character implicated in society which is so essential to the novel. Most of the major characters of *Amelia,* with the exception of the worst villains, are on the lookout for exquisite feelings: that is why they are willing audiences to each other's lengthy narratives, so that they can participate in the evocation of what they themselves self-consciously refer to as "tender scenes." Even the beloved husband of a beloved wife does not rest happy in his matrimonial state without seeking moments when conjugal affection can be concentrated in exquisite sensation: Booth says of Balligard, the Frenchman who he learns had designs on his wife, "To say the truth, I afterward thought myself almost obliged to him for a meeting with Amelia the most luxuriously delicate that can be imagined" (III, 9). "Luxurious delicacy" is the kind of phrase which in the earlier novels is used with a cunning satiric doubleness, to indicate, say, the carnal propensities of a Bridget Allworthy, but here there is no suspicion of irony.

One of the most revealing expressions of the shift in attitude toward sensation in Fielding's last novel is the peculiar fact of Amelia's feminine debility. In his earlier fiction, Fielding had been particularly happy in representing virtuous women who were vigorously energetic, and he gave only a few hints of a possible assent to the new literary fashion of polarizing humanity into rough though tamable males and delicate, hypersensitive, spiritually finer females. Amelia does retain a certain resiliency or at least forbearance in adversity, but she also exhibits a delicate female sensibility which registers small shocks as major quakes and brings her to the inevitable verge of fainting at several points in the novel. It may well be that Fielding was influenced by Richardson in this respect. He had been immensely impressed by *Clarissa,* which appeared three years before *Amelia,* and he may even have wanted to suggest he intended a more Richardsonian kind of novel by adopting the practice of Richardson's two published novels in using a virtuous heroine's name for the title.[5] In any case, the congenital debility of the virtuous female plausibly follows from the assumptions of the novel of sensibility: virtue itself is ultimately determined by the degree to which the character's heart is "sensible," in the eighteenth-century sense of the term, and so the character that is to be the model of virtue is likely to possess an instrument of response to experience which is exquisitely sensitive and therefore somewhat fragile as well. All this heightened interest, then, in intense and supposedly virtuous sensations encourages schematic simplifications of human nature in the novel and leads the novelist away from the sphere most congenial to him—the solid, multifaceted, variously populated social world—into a private domain not so much of feeling as of the delectation of feeling, where language itself becomes a violation of the purity of emotion.

I do not want to suggest that *Amelia* is in any consistent
way a novel of sensibility, or that the insistently didactic
notes to which we have attended ring through the entire
structure of the book. Most of what Fielding does in his
last novel, bad and good alike, is done in spots and patches,
and if this contributes to making *Amelia* a miscarried novel
in some important respects, it means that the faults are not
unrelieved. *Amelia* is certainly very far from being a general
failure, unless we foolishly expect, as some critics have done,
that it be another *Tom Jones*, something which Fielding
himself clearly did not intend. It is not enough to say there
are good things in *Amelia;* there are things in this book
which one simply does not find in the English novel until it
reaches a stage of greater technical sophistication, in the
nineteenth century.

To begin with, Fielding's only partially successful attempt
at making the novel a vehicle of practical, panoramic criticism of contemporary society is unique in kind until the end
of the century. This aspect of Fielding's achievement against
the background of his own age is brought into sharp relief
by the tone and tendency of Richardson's expressed disapproval of *Amelia:*

> I have not been able to read more than the first volume of Amelia.
> Poor Fielding! I could not help telling his sister, that I was equally
> surprised at and concerned for his continued lowness. Had your
> brother, said I, been born in a stable, or been a runner at a spong-
> ing house, we should have thought him a genius, and wished he had
> the advantage of a liberal education, and of being admitted into
> good company; but it's beyond my conception, that a man of good
> family, and who had some learning, and who really is a writer, should
> descend so excessively low in all his pieces. Who can care for any of
> his low people? [6]

Such appalling condescension was not, of course, typical
of all eighteenth-century readers, but it does point up the

real advantages as a novelist that Fielding's own social background and temperament gave him. For Richardson's distressingly narrow range of social and moral sympathy is precisely the opposite of the quality we like to associate with the novel as a genre. A profoundly bourgeois sensibility like Richardson's could contribute to the extension of realism downward, into the inner depths, but not outward, in social space. The rise of the novel is, of course, historically connected with the rise of the middle class; but—as the Goncourts argued in their preface to *Germanie Lacerteux*—it may be equally legitimate to consider the novel as the democratic rather than the bourgeois genre, impelled by a sense of responsibility to extend the "franchise" of realistic representation to the underprivileged classes, the despised occupations, the neglected social settings. Fielding, to be sure, presents his lower-class people sympathetically but always from a carefully maintained distance—his final imaginative allegiance is to the traditional values of the landed gentry. He is free, however, of the constant uneasiness about social standing which in a self-made man like Richardson produces such morally paralyzing snobbery.

What disgusted Richardson in *Amelia* belongs to the very substance of its original achievement. Fielding thrusts us into "low" settings like Newgate and the bailiff's house not so much in the manner of Smollett, who used such locations to pay off personal scores and to tie together formal satiric vignettes, as in the manner of the later Dickens, for whom the institutions of justice and detention were vivid illustrations and symbolic embodiments of the pervasive, maddening perversity of society at large. Social panorama is clearly essential to Fielding's purpose in *Amelia*. He had also been interested in social panorama in his two previous novels, but here the lines of connection between the various parts of the big picture are drawn tighter. The noblemen and the turnkeys of *Amelia* are linked not only by a common moral posture—as, say, noblewoman and country wench are connected in *Tom Jones*—but also by the common role they play, at different levels, as functionaries of the same utterly cynical system of social and legal power. Fielding had perhaps given an intimation of this general approach in *Jonathan Wild*, but he makes its social implications more apparent in *Amelia* and comes closer to a particularized observation of contemporary institutions and practices.

Equally important, there are sections of *Amelia* which demonstrate that Fielding could attain a new subtlety in the presentation of character by leaving most of the commentary to the reader's imagination while preserving the ample balance achieved in his comic novels between shrewd satiric observation and humanely sympathetic imagination. The long encounter in prison between Booth and Miss Matthews (Books, I, II, III, and the beginning of IV) is a tour de force of a sort scarcely attempted in the English novel for another century, and it nicely illustrates how Fielding was developing a new mode of fiction out of his old methods. The two regressive narratives—first Miss Matthews', then Booth's—derive technically from the interpolated tales of the comic novels, and may seem a little cumbersome to certain readers, but in their manner of drawing us dramatically into the lives of the protagonists, they anticipate the flashback techniques of later fiction, introducing the substance of the main action and not merely offering an analogy to it.

Necessary information is gradually disclosed with a fine sense of timing. At first, we are not even told that Booth is married; the first mention of it is from the mouth of Miss Matthews. Then Miss Matthews, still a somewhat enigmatic presence for the reader, recounts in detail her own fall from virtue, and finally we get to Booth and his tale of Amelia and their courtship and marriage. While all this rehearsal of the past is going on, Fielding uses a quieter, subtler version of the technique of breaking in upon interpolations which we observed in *Joseph Andrews* and *Tom Jones:* as the two old friends talk on in the privacy of Miss Matthews' cell, it slowly dawns on us that her sympathy for him is excessively animated, that she has a particular interest in him, that she is ogling him, that she is offering her immediate, experienced services as substitute wife. In the interplay, moreover, between genial naif and congenial seductress, Fielding manages to maintain a nice balance of affectionate sympathy and satiric censure for both, so contriving the adulterous liaison that we can see its origins in a most understandable human weakness together with its morally reprehensible implications and even its comic aspects.

In the splendid figure of Miss Matthews, who lamentably is reduced later in the novel for didactic reasons to a venomous Rejected Mistress, Fielding hints at an ironic doubleness of attitude toward that very pursuit of sentiment which is undertaken elsewhere in the novel with distressing single-mindedness. Miss Matthews is presented to us as a reader, or rather listener, of sensibility par excellence. When Booth offers to omit from his narrative the description of a particularly tender scene between him and Amelia, she protests vehemently: "Indeed I beg you will not . . . nothing delights me more than scenes of tenderness. I should be glad to know, if possible, every syllable which was uttered on both sides" (III, 1). The effect of attributing this delight in tender scenes to Miss Matthews of all people, given her past history and present motives, is to cast a teasing shadow of suspicion over the whole mode of sensibility which the writer himself seems to relish. Booth, invoking a familiar formula as he recalls Amelia's fainting at his first declaration of love, tells Miss Matthews, "To describe my sensation till she returned to herself is not in my power." And his listener's response would seem to illustrate nicely the dogma of sensibility that a word to the wise heart is always sufficient: " 'You need not,' cried Miss Matthews. 'Oh, happy Amelia! why had not I been blessed with such a passion?' " (II, 2). Does Miss Matthews have a sensible heart, or merely the superficial empathy of an envious one, the keen imagination of unsated desire? Fielding exercises sound artistic tact in leaving the doubt suspended as Miss Matthews goes on to suggest obliquely—she dares do no more—that the nobility of Booth's passion exceeds the worthiness of the object it has chosen in Amelia.

Just a little further on in Booth's narrative (II, 4), the doubt about the candor of Miss Matthews' tender heart is almost resolved. Booth again apologizes for the ineffability of an experience, this time, having his beloved sister die in his arms: " 'The sensations I felt are to be known only from experience, and to you must appear dull and insipid' . . . Here Mr. Booth stopped a moment, and wiped his eyes; and Miss Matthews, perhaps out of complaisance, wiped hers." The characteristic strategy of the double irony in *Tom Jones* is here interestingly reversed. The narrator of *Tom Jones* would probably have had Miss Matthews wipe her eyes "perhaps out of tender sympathy," a pointed irony which would lead us to infer that the character's motive was quite the opposite—or possibly, quite the opposite of the asserted motive and yet just a little like it. The "perhaps" phrase which Fielding actually uses here evokes a similar suspension of absolute judgment, but with a shift in emphasis from satiric exposure to sympathetic reconsideration. In *Amelia*, Fielding is not interested in maintaining a consistent ironic elevation over his personages, and so here he states directly what we are by now prepared to infer in any case —that Miss Matthews' tears are a show put on for Booth. But—the strategic "perhaps" makes us wonder—are they entirely that? We have already been given enough hints to guess that Miss Matthews throughout is preparing the way for the seduction of Booth, but, at least in this first part of the novel, she shows a warm sympathy and generosity which probably cannot be wholly explained away as strategems of seduction. In the new, subdued presentation of character in

Amelia, then, Fielding gives us a chastened version of his familiar inferential technique which leads us at once to a firm moral judgment of character and a tolerant recognition of the mixed nature of human motives.

As the narrator tends to withdraw from the action in *Amelia,* much of the inferential activity which is evoked by authorial comment in *Tom Jones* is now shifted to the uninterrupted exchanges between the characters. The novel, in short, becomes more purely dramatic. The best moments, for example, in the dialogue between Booth and Miss Matthews exhibit a deftness of comic revelation and a bold dramatic irony unparalleled in the earlier novels. Here is Miss Matthews, indignant over the discovery that Mandeville makes no provision in his philosophy for the greatest of passions:

> "If he denies there is any such thing as love, that is most certainly wrong. I am afraid I can give him the lie myself."
> "I will join with you, madam, in that," answered Booth, "at any time."
> "Will you join with me?" answered she, looking eagerly at him— "O, Mr. Booth! I know not what I was going to say—What—Where did you leave off? I would not interrupt you—but I am impatient to know something."
> "What, madam?" cries Booth; "if I can give you any satisfaction—"
> "No, no," said she, "I must hear all; I would not for the world break the thread of your story. Besides, I am afraid to ask—Pray, pray, sir, go on." (III, 5)

A beautifully transparent exposure of character and motive is achieved here through the most natural exchange of speech, with none of the manifest stylization or comic heightening of dialogue we noted in *Joseph Andrews* and *Tom Jones.* In the absence of the narrator, the characters assume a new independence: we know them for what they are by what they say and think, how each responds to what is said and apparently thought by the other. The nature of the relationship between Miss Matthews and Booth, which has been revealed in stages through their long colloquy, is suddenly thrown into sharp focus by Booth's inadvertent double entendre: Miss Matthews pounces on the sexual implication with joyful anticipation, then, confused in her excitement, hesitant at having moved too soon, she quickly retreats, while the inveterately well-meaning, unsuspecting Booth sails blithely on to still another unwitting sexual pun, promising to give his warm-tempered female companion "any satisfaction." Sterne sometimes works double entendre into dialogue in similar fashion, but without the same developing interplay of character that culminates in the comic exchange here. To find dialogue in an English novel that can generate this kind of revealing, limpidly dramatic irony, one has to look to Jane Austen and beyond. As with other artistic virtues of *Amelia,* it is something that comes in flashes, not as a steady illumination, but its very presence in the book is an indication of the author's undiminished originality and technical command.

Fielding's last novel, in sum, with all its obvious unevenness, is still the work of a writer of genius; it offers some striking evidence that he was beginning, however uncertainly, to explore bold new possibilities for the genre he himself had already helped to bring to a brilliant first maturity. However, because Fielding was to leave *Amelia* without an artistic sequel, his new aims in it only partly realized, this last novel remains, finally, a fascinating and instructive anomaly. It is to *Joseph Andrews* and *Tom Jones* that we must look for the vividly achieved models of what could be made of this protean form called the novel by a writer balancing the claims of literary tradition and contemporary reality, of adherence to moral actuality in all its unseemly blemishes and devotion to the lovely unity of a perfected art.

We should use definition in the end in order to surround the indefinable. If you "define" the novel or the sonnet you will not be able to read the next one that alters the limits.
—R. P. Blackmur,
A Primer of Ignorance

6. FIELDING AND THE FUTURE OF THE NOVEL

The novel as a genre seems to bear within it not the seeds of its own destruction but rather the repeated threat, repeatedly unfulfilled, of its own imminent demise. In England, the necrologists of the novel were at work as early as the 1790's, predicting the final collapse of that new literary form which, after having drawn a deep breath of life from Fielding, Richardson, Smollett, and Sterne, had puffed itself up to the turgidities of the Gothic tale and the tremulous vacuities of the novel of sensibility. During the nineteenth century, the great age of heroic expansion of the genre, such predictions, though not entirely silenced by contemporary accomplishments, were heard less frequently; but in our own century, for reasons both obvious and devious, the voices prophesying doom to the genre have been more numerous, more insistent, more resonant.

The novel in various places has gone through cycles of intense creativity and relative decline: the extraordinary achievements, produced by a complicated conjunction of historical circumstance and coincidental genius, in England from 1740 to 1771, in England and France from 1830 to 1871, in Russia from 1861 to 1905, in France, Germany, England, and America in the 1920's, made the various periods that followed look to some observers like the beginning of the end. This dim view of the future of the genre has been especially encouraged by the propensity of the novel to shatter its own conventions, transcend its own limits, transform its nature in the most unexpected and sometimes seemingly perverse ways. The novel as we knew it and cherished it is almost always dying: while we sadly contemplate the cooling ashes of the splendid past, it may be hard for us to recognize in the improbable-looking chick poking its head out of the rubble the next avatar of the phoenix.

In obituaries of the novel, the cause of death is usually assigned to one of two general categories—either to a process of growth and decline inherent in the genre, or to the changing nature of the reality which is to be represented by the genre. That is to say, either the generic possibilities of the novel have been "exhausted" in the achievements of the great novelists—this, for example, is the gist of Ortega y Gasset's argument in his "Notes on the Novel" [1]—or the social world we inhabit, the movement of history in which we are immersed, have assumed forms that are radically resistant to novelistic representation. The second of these two explanations of the novel's decline obviously has greatest bearing on the novelistic tradition of social realism; the notion of exhausted possibilities, on the other hand, seems to me to be more particularly relevant to the rendering of consciousness in the novel.

In both instances, Fielding provides a useful starting point for thinking about alternatives that may still be open to the novelist. It should be obvious enough that Fielding is hardly a figure from whom contemporary writers are likely to "learn" in any direct or explicit way. However much our contemporary we may want to make him, his place is conspicuously at the other end of the history of the novel, before most of

the great masters of the genre had done their work, before
the face of reality was darkened and twisted by the horrors
and confusions of modern experience. But precisely because
his practice is so strikingly different from what has been, by
and large, the prevailing practice of novelists over the past
century and more, his achievement may adumbrate possibilities of fiction more viable today than quotidian social realism,
and as illuminating in their own fashion as the detailed trans-
scription of consciousness. In order to see what relevance
Fielding might have to the contemporary predicament, it
may be useful to look back briefly on a major line of development in the traditional novel.

One of many possible ways—each in itself necessarily incomplete—of viewing the history of the novel is as a dialectic between
consciousness and things, between personality and the world of
unyielding objects that impinges upon it. There is no dialectic of
this sort in the older narrative forms because they generally
reflect a sense of organic connection between man and the things
with which he lives. The epic warrior's armor and weapons, the
faithful lady's distaff, are perfect extensions of the self, often, in
fact, divinely appointed: it is supremely right that Achilles'
shield, fashioned for him by the god, should unite heaven and
earth, war and peace, the stance of battle with the cycle of the
year and the harmony of the cosmos. Since the Renaissance, this
sense, or perhaps dream, of organic connection between man and
things has been ruptured. Hegel and the Marxists after him
are surely right in seeing the Industrial Revolution as a major
force in alienating men from their own implements, but the
process of alienation had begun long before the Industrial
Revolution, with the disorienting changes not only in the
social and economic order but also in the inner structures
of scientific knowledge and belief in the sixteenth and seven-
teenth centuries. The novel begins at the turn of the seven-
teenth century when a would-be hero's imagination tries to
resist the unredeemed neutrality, the sodden gayness, of the alien

things that surround him: his heroism consists in his brave, pathetic, noble, and of course mad attempt to force the indifferent things of his world into consonance with his own heroic ideals—basins into helmets, windmills into dragons, broken-winded nags into fiery steeds.

The explicit pattern of *Don Quixote* was repeated in many novels, but even where it was not, a kind of tense interplay between people and things persisted. Human figures were often approached through the layers of things they seemed almost to secrete all around them and through the marks and stains of usage they left upon things. The famous description of the Maison Vauquer at the beginning of *Le Père Goriot* is a paradigm for this mode of representation which, in different forms, appears in Flaubert, George Eliot, Trollope, Zola, Bennett, the earlier Thomas Mann, and many other novelists. Conversely, the traditional novel often conceived personality as shaped or sustained by things, hedged about by them, embedded in them, impaled upon them. Dickens gives one of the most powerful expressions to this uneasy dialectic between people and things by creating a world where, as Dorothy Van Ghent and others have noted, the two sides often exchange places, things, as though daemonically possessed, assuming the vitality and character of people while people take on the rigidity, sometimes even the deadness, of things.

Dickens, by imagining the interplay between men and things with such hallucinated intensity, brings his "realistic" fiction to the brink of comic fantasia or, in the later novels, to the brink of nightmare. Kafka, deeply influenced by Dickens, cuts away the moorings of quotidian reality and re-creates the world as an inscrutable and often terrifying wonderland of expressionistic fiction. His peculiar achievement, which no writer since has been able really to build upon successfully, is a symptom of one of the predicaments of the twentieth-century novel: in an existence that repeatedly dissolves into nightmare, both private and public, the old cluttered world of familiar things out of which novels once were made no longer seems very believable. Mary Mc-Carthy, in "The Fact in Fiction," one of the most intelligent obituaries written for the novel in recent years, makes the point succinctly: "The novel, with its common sense, is of all forms the least adapted to encompass the modern world, whose leading characteristic is irreality." [2] Especially after the total eclipse of humanity in the last World War, the mind does not easily hold its grip on familiar things. The merest household objects—lampshades, soap—can become triggers of horror; the associations of a word like "skin"—the roughness or fineness of which was once a social index in the novel—may easily be screened by darker thoughts of radiation burns and napalm.

Violence and horror, I should add, are not the only aspects of "irreality" with which the contemporary world confronts us. There is a disturbing factitiousness—a profoundly unsettling sameness and characterless interchangeability—that clings to the mass-produced things with which we live. In Dickens' world or Zola's, things, in their very ugliness and dirtiness and peculiarity, could be seen in significant relation to individual character; in our own world, it often seems as though everything were made out of the same hollow plastic, mechanically molded, whatever its use, in the same "modernistic" patterns. No one has written more passionately or more eloquently on this subject than Norman Mailer; his criticism of contemporary architecture, a brief passage of which I offer here, vividly suggests one reason why novels can no longer be easily written in the old way:

The essence of totalitarianism is that it beheads. It beheads individuality, variety, dissent, extreme possibility, romantic faith; it blinds vision, deadens instinct; it obliterates the past. It makes factories look like college campuses or mental hospitals, where once factories had the specific beauty of revealing their huge and sometimes brutal function. It makes the new buildings on college campuses look like factories . . . The flat surfaces, blank ornamentation, and pastel colors of the new schoolhouses will maroon . . . children in an endless hallway of the present. The totalitarian impulse not only washes away distinctions but looks for a style in buildings, in clothing, and in the ornamentation of tools, appliances, and daily objects which will diminish one's sense of function and reduce one's sense of reality by reducing such emotions as awe, dread, beauty, pity, terror, calm, horror, and harmony. By dislocating us from the most powerful emotions of reality, totalitarianism leaves us further isolated in the empty landscapes of psychosis.[3]

The empty landscapes of psychosis are obviously no place in which to write a *Middlemarch* or a *Buddenbrooks*. I say this not out of nostalgia for the solid social novels of the past but merely to underscore our own particular predicament; for the novels that render haunted inner landscapes, the very books we think of as paradigmatically modern, can, like the older social novels, illuminate our common human condition or merely expose at tedious lenght their authors' lack of moral and artistic imagination. What is important to keep in mind is the difficulty that the contemporary novelist often has in engaging the social world, in making it body forth the nuances and complexities and knotty idiosyncrasies of character. The blurring of distinctions between different institutions and different milieux to which Mailer alludes deprives the social novel of a major root system in the soil of social reality: some latter-day Dickens or Zola trying to write a *Hard Times* or *Germinal* might well end up with a book that showed suspicious affinities with the many contemporary novels of academic life, not only in the glass-walled, fluorescent-lighted settings, but in the enclosed bureaucratic ethic common to both industrial and educational institutions in our society.

Equally problematic for the novelist is the obliteration of the past in the artifacts of mass-produced culture, that general experience of being marooned, as Mailer tellingly puts it, "in an endless hallway of the present." One of the most effective methods in the traditional social novel for representing individual character and class values was through the description of the material accretions of past experience still visible, still used, in the present. To cite an early but seminal example, when Scott in *Rob Roy* introduces us to the Northumberland estate of the Vernons, he gives us the most concrete sense of the life and history of a family by focusing on the material possessions with which they have lived for generations: in the paintings darkened by a century of hearth-fire smoke, in the massive oaken fixtures, in the remnants of old armor, we can feel the presence of generations of Vernons, we can infer what kind of people they are, what their culture has been.

The contemporary novelist, on the other hand, if he wants to reveal the life style of his personages through their domestic furnishings, is generally confronted with more limiting materials: the infinitely reduplicated and vulgarized Danish modern; the various popular versions of Hollywood rococo (gilded curlicue ornamentation, vast serpentine sofas, ubiquitous gold flecks in upholstery, carpeting, and in formica surfaces); or some related style invented just yesterday by the manufacturers, cut off from any meaningful relationship with the past and with individual taste. This standardization and isolation in time of our cultural artifacts may be one reason for the thinness and triteness, the peculiar quality of tedious inconsequentiality, of many novels that have employed the methods of conventional social realism in recent years. I of course do not mean to suggest that it is now impossible for a novelist to reveal character and values convincingly through the description of material possessions. Obviously, people still exercise personal taste, even in our so-called mass society. It should be equally obvious, however, that personal taste in such a society is often subtly compromised when not actually subverted by mass standards. In the traditional novel, moreover, individual taste is intimately related to class values, an association that becomes somewhat less probable for the fiction of an age in which class styles, if not class distinctions, are gradually eroded or confused.

It is clear that this whole notion of fiction founded on a minutely realized world of familiar things, and of a dialectic between things and consciousness, has nothing to do with Fielding. Although in the traditional critical account, which goes back to Scott and ultimately to Johnson, Fielding is thought of as a "painter of national manners," there are few detailed social discriminations in his work and certainly nothing of the patient accumulation of particulars of milieu which we associate with the amplitude of the great social realists. In point of fact, he is drastically selective with social materials, boldly summarizing, deleting, in a sense even abstracting from the contemporary world which is supposed to be "represented," realistically, in his fiction. We expect, for example, a finely calibrated time scale in the novel, the narrative progressing from moment to moment as the protagonists live onward, but Fielding creates a credible version of contemporary experience with nothing of the sort. The presence of a commenting narrator gives the impression of leisurely progress in his novels, while he actually uses two very different time scales for the narration of events—a purely dramatic one, in which the spoken exchanges between characters, and any conspicuous physical action attendant upon those exchanges, take up more or less the time they would require to act out; and a much broader scale, in which long and complicated series of actions "occur" in a sentence or two, or perhaps in a paragraph.

If a *trompe l'oeil* effect is intrinsic to many novels—the image painted so meticulously that we take it for the real object—Fielding's world comes to life rather through a magnificent sleight of hand: the prestidigitator's touch is so sure that if he shows us but the corner of an ear, nicely positioned, we are quite ready to believe that he has the rest of the real rabbit up his voluminous sleeve. Perhaps this is finally why Fielding remains, as a character of Kingsley Amis is made to reflect, "the only non-contemporary novelist who could be read with unaffected and whole-hearted interest, the only one who never had to be excused on the grounds of changing taste"[4]—because the world he portrays subsists in the lucent medium of the narrator's intelligence, not in the verbal simulacra of all the bricks and clapboards and gingham and lace which were the stuff of reality at a certain point in time.

Over against Virginia Woolf's parable of Mr. Bennett and Mrs. Brown in the railway coach, the life of the old lady escaping in the catalog of buttons and buckles through which Mr. Bennett would describe her, we might usefully set this account in *Tom Jones* of a man and woman on a stagecoach journey: "Now there was a certain office in the gift of Mr. Fitzpatrick at that time vacant, namely, that of a wife; for the lady who had lately filled that office had resigned, or at least deserted her duty. Mr. Fitzpatrick therefore, having thoroughly examined Mrs. Waters on the road, found her extremely fit for the place, which, on their arrival at Bath, he presently conferred upon her, and she without any scruple accepted" (XVII, 9). Without the clatter of carriage wheels and the creak of old leather springs or the crack of the coachman's whip, without the long hours of conversation— verbal or otherwise—between the two travelers, Mr. Fitzpatrick and Mrs. Waters are as vivid when we encounter them now on the printed page as the day they were invented. Our interests in, or understanding of, external realities may change, but our delight in the play of ironic intelligence over human motives and actions has not diminished in two centuries: for us, as must have been true for Fielding's first readers, too, the human situation leaps to life through our very pleasure in inferring it from the teasing indirection of the language—which invites us to imagine Mr. Fitzpatrick's quick inclinations, Mrs. Waters' habitual responsiveness, the nature of the thorough examination in the coach for the office of wife and Mrs. Waters' demonstration of her extreme fitness for that important position. The life of Fielding's novels will fade only when the colors of the English language so fade that the implications of the words he chooses become unrecognizable.

The preponderance of comic novels in England and especially in America since the early 1950's, the renewed interest among writers in the possibilities of ironic fiction, suggest that Fielding may have fresh relevance to the present literary situation. When actuality begins to seem recalcitrant or even repellent to the novelist's imagination, it is understandable that the novel should in many instances become broadly reflexive, examining or displaying the instruments of representation as it represents experience. In an age of moral confusions, when the social world itself sometimes seems not quite imaginable, the novelist may find the self-conscious operation of his own literary intelligence the surest material he has to work with. The many novels about the writing of novels, from Gide and Proust to Durrell and Amis, the novels in which the principal observer is always aware of himself observing and formulating, often against a background of literary precedents—these all possess an ultimate affinity with Fielding's ironic, self-conscious, theorizing narrator and with the even more self-conscious, magnificently self-defeating narrator of his great successor, Sterne.

One manifestation in some serious writers of this general reflexive movement of the novel has been a very special emphasis on style. Thorough-going stylization, to be sure, tends to have more radical metaphysical implications for modern novelists than it did for Fielding: in Joyce, in Proust, in Durrell, and, more playfully, in Nabokov, the artful recasting of language implies a rival creation, the establishment through words of a world that is in some sense superior to the world of ordinary existence. Nevertheless, Fielding provides the first signal instance of a novelist transfiguring the world of his fiction through style, never shrinking from the boldest contrasts between the harmonious perfection of the style and the imperfect nature of the world the style conveys. If one's notion of the novel is derived primarily from figures like Richardson and Defoe, it becomes difficult to encompass critically achievements like that of the great Hebrew novelist S. Y. Agnon, who writes about the awful dislocations and dissonances of the twentieth century in a beautifully crafted Hebrew that is basically medieval, occasionally even biblical.

Agnon's linguistic practice is an extreme illustration of what remains an underlying aspect of stylization in the novel: because language develops slowly in time, and most spectacularly through literature, any writer who tries to utilize the full resources of his language will inevitably allude, in his vocabulary, in his rhetoric, perhaps even in his grammar and syntax, to the history of the language and the literature of the past. That is to say, implicit in the very act of stylization is a kind of linguistic "agenbite of inwit," in the memorable phrase Joyce resuscitated, characteristically, from a fourteenth-century moral treatise. Style itself, then, can become a window through which the rich and variegated light of the past floods into that endless hallway of the present. Fielding's two comic novels are the first great models for this relationship between style and contemporary reality. In striking contrast to Richardson, he refuses to represent the contemporary world solely in its own linguistic and cultural terms; instead, he creates a style which, like the best allusive poetry of Dryden and Pope, invokes—in a sense, recapitulates —a whole spectrum of European civilization from Homer and Horace to the French neoclassicists and the eighteenth-century English essayists.

Let me stress once more that I am not suggesting equations or direct influences in comparing modern novelists to Fielding: what concerns us here are affinities, perhaps partial, but, it seems to me, instructive nevertheless. The novelists of our century in general, even the greatest of them, have suffered from a lack which the late R. P. Blackmur attributed to Proust and Faulkner in particular—the "absence of syntax, the power of composing or arranging things, giving them ordinance, so that their parts are in living relation to the intelligence." [5] Fielding, on the other hand, as I have tried to make clear in the course of this study, possessed syntax above all else, in the comprehensive sense in which Blackmur uses that term: it is the very substance of his genius, the universal key to his artistic practice. The masterful syntax of a *Tom Jones* is not feasible for novelists today for the obvious reason that they can no longer believe in the nice correspondence between intelligence and reality which was the precondition for Fielding's architectonic strength, for his unfailing coherence of purpose and technique. Omniscient narrators are rare nowadays because writers cannot really believe that any mind can embrace and control reality in the grand old manner. Such affinities with Fielding, therefore, as one may find in modern fiction tend to be refracted affinities. Allusive, avowedly stylized, or "literary" representations of experience occur in novels that are deliberately fragmented, disordered, confused—broken mirrors of a broken world. Self-dramatizing, self-parodying, self-ironic narrators are included in the action and so are excluded from the privileges of authorial overview.

This last transformation of the self-conscious, ironic mode of fiction which Fielding initiated suggests an interesting general alternative to the verisimilar transcription of consciousness in the novel. We have been so close to consciousness for so long that it has become something of a bore, at least in the hands of many contemporary novelists. After the brilliant illuminations of consciousness by Joyce, Proust, and Faulkner, writers often seem to be reduced to tired imitations, or to focusing on odd peripheries or restricted strips of consciousness (as, for example, in the work of Nathalie Sarraute and Alain Robbe-Grillet). In any case, the feel of one's own experience from within is only one major aspect of human reality, not the total reality. We need not assent to the dogmatic artistic conservatism of a C. P. Snow in order to accord some validity to his assertion that the so-called psychological novel is often deficient in "causal psychological insight . . . that is, not the insight which tells us what it is to be in a certain mood . . . but the insight which probes beneath the continuum of feeling and asks, 'Why should I, of all people, have this mood at all? be driven by these motives? be capable of this action? live this unique life?' " [6] Fielding's kind of novel, because it is not minutely analytical in the manner of the nineteenth-century novels Sir Charles seems to have in mind, does not always afford adequate answers to these large questions, but the double perspectives of its irony sometimes do allow us, as we have seen, an access to character that is simultaneous with a critical view of character from without, against a large background of astutely perceived moral and social experience.

With the hope of showing more clearly what bearing Fielding's achievement can have on the possibilities of the novel in the twentieth century, I am going to set end to end four passages from four very different novels, with some brief commentary on each. In three of the passages we see a lover contemplating the object of his desires, from the excited viewpoint of the lover himself. In the passage from Fielding, it is the woman who regards the man with the hot eyes of desire, while the viewpoint is not that of either of the actors in the scene.

It is well to begin with Richardson, since he is so clearly the initiator of a central tradition in the novel. I quote from near the beginning of the letter in *Clarissa* dated "Tuesday, Wedn., April 11, 12"; Lovelace is describing the moment when Clarissa steps through the door of the garden wall, thus falling into his trap and allowing him to abscond with her:

The moment I heard the door unbolt I was sure of her. That motion made my heart bound to my throat. But when that was followed with the presence of my charmer, flashing upon me all at once in a flood of brightness, sweetly dressed, though all unprepared for a journey, I trod air, and hardly thought myself a mortal.

I have told thee what were *my* transports, when the undrawn bolt presented to me my long-expected goddess. *Her* emotions were more sweetly feminine after the first moments; for then the fire of her starry eyes began to sink into a less dazzling languor. She trembled: nor knew she how to support the agitations of a heart she had never found so ungovernable. She was even fainting, when I clasped her in my supporting arms. What a precious moment that! How near, how sweetly near, the throbbing partners!

After more than two centuries, it may be difficult for us to recapture the exciting newness of this kind of writing in its own time, the extraordinary breakthrough in the literary representation of experience it constituted. Even what may seem stale or contrived in the vocabulary of the two paragraphs—"charmer," "goddess," "starry eyes"—reflects with perfect fidelity the mental and cultural style of the speaker, a man who lives with and by the tag ends of Cavalier amorous verse and its post-Restoration successors. The passage, quite brilliantly, is all moments and emotions. Narration progresses from instant to instant—the click of the bolt, the appearance of Clarissa—with tiny erratic jumps forward in the continuum of time as Lovelace's stirred emotions (recollected in anything but tranquility) leap from one high moment of recalled intensity to another. There is no attempt to describe the "objective" appearance of external realities, only a rendering of the impact of their assault on Lovelace's senses. We do not see Clarissa actually stepping through the door: instead we are given the sudden explosion of her presence upon Lovelace's tautly wound expectation; her "flashing upon [him] all at once in a flood of brightness" is more a record of immediate apprehension than a conscious poetic hyperbole. The modifier "sweetly" invoked three times in the two paragraphs, always adverbially, reflects the focus of representation in the writing: it is on the modifications of feeling as it is being felt, the particular sensuous tinges that attach to acts and stances in the mind of the protagonist. Lovelace's closeness to his recently experienced emotions merges at the end of the passage with his physical closeness to Clarissa—the throbbing partners clasped heart to heart—and so his report of his own consciousness culminates, as it does so often in this novel, in a swoon of desire.

This close representation of experience through consciousness has been so thoroughly absorbed into Western literary sensibility, is so naturally accessible to everyone from Virginia Woolf to the common pornographer, that one can hardly speak of "influence" in Richardson's case. Before we go on, however, to examine a passage from a later work that stands in the same novelistic tradition as Richardson, we might briefly look at a scene from *Joseph Andrews*. Lady Booby, alone with Joseph in her bedroom, has been coyly dangling before him the notion that she might allow him to kiss her, and she finally persuades him to tell her what he would think of his lady if she permitted him such an intimacy:

"Madam," said Joseph, "I should think your ladyship condescended a great deal below yourself." "Pugh!" said she, "that I am to answer to myself: but would not you insist on more? Would you be contented with a kiss? Would not your inclinations be all on fire rather by such a favour?" "Madam," said Joseph, "if they were, I hope I should be able to control them, without suffering them to get the better of my virtue."—You have heard, reader, poets talk of the "statue of Surprise"; you have heard likewise, or else you have heard very little, how Surprise made one of the sons of Croesus speak, though he was dumb. You have seen the faces, in the eighteen-penny gallery, when, through the trap-door, to soft or no music, Mr. Bridgewater, Mr. William Mills, or some other of ghostly appearance, hath ascended, with a face all pale with powder, and a shirt all bloody with ribbons; but from none of these, nor from Phidias, or Praxiteles, if they should return to life—no, not from the inimitable pencil of my friend Hogarth, could you receive such an idea of Surprise as would have entered in at your eyes had they beheld the Lady Booby when those

last words issued out from the lips of Joseph.—"Your virtue!" (said
the lady, recovering after a silence of two minutes) "I shall never
survive it. Your virtue!" (I, 8)

The exchange between the innocent Joseph and his eager
lady is dramatic in the strict sense of the term—instructively,
a reference to the contemporary theater, in fact to two actors
who played roles in Fielding's comedies, is given emphasis
in the long authorial interpolation. The narrator makes no
pretense to immediacy in conveying the encounter to us;
on the contrary, he calls our attention to the fact that we
are not actual spectators at this scene (the idea of Surprise
"*would* have entered in at your eyes *had* they beheld Lady
Booby"), only witnesses to his own re-creation of it. The
interruption of the dialogue that begins with "You have
heard, reader," is a marvelously effective "camera-stopping"
technique that builds up comic suspense before the climactic
explosion of Lady Booby's indignant "Your virtue!" Fielding
wants us to notice that he has set himself two minutes of
silence to fill in. A writer of Richardsonian inclinations might
have evoked the passage of that time by plunging us into
the vortex of the thwarted lady's emotions, suggesting through
a series of mental stammerings and fragmentary thoughts
her incredulity, confusion, astonishment, outrage. What Fielding does instead is to make the self-conscious activity of the
narrator, who stands, as it were, between us and the stage
of action, an integral part of the novelistic event.

The ironic focus upon this modern wife of Potiphar and
her Joseph is sharpened by setting her image against a whole
range of other possible imitations of reality, in various media,
from Greek sculpture and Latin poetry or its modern successors
to the contrived tragic effects of the contemporary stage and the
engravings of Hogarth. At this solemn moment of Lady Booby's
rejection, as a terrible blow is struck against the most tender
part of her sexual and social pride, Fielding shrinks her swollen
feelings to comic dimensions by reminding us that we are readers

(who, unless we "have heard very little," ought to know our Herodotus!), that the story is a story, and that its actors belong somewhere near the bottom of the great scale of art that runs from the sublime to the ridiculous, from Phidias to the trap doors and powdered faces of the Haymarket theater. The Richardsonian presentation of experience aims at re-creating its affective dimension and thus sometimes reproduces a kind of scrambling of apprehension, a *dérèglement de tous les sens,* because of the excited erotic nature of the experience. Fielding's dramatic-ironic method, by contrast, has the effect of "grounding" the erotic electricity implict in the situation while illuminating the comic possibilities of the sexual encounter against a background of cultural tradition and moral valuation.

For a long time after Fielding, this particular mode of fiction was followed by very few novelists of stature, in England or elsewhere. Sterne develops some of its extreme possibilities; Diderot imitates aspects of it at one remove, 'through the happy intermediary of Sterne; Thackeray, a great talent hampered by the artistic and moral inhibitions of his period, applies it unevenly though on occasion brilliantly. The mainstream of the novel however, certainly from the middle of the nineteenth century, flowed in the channel first cut out by Richardson. A passage like the one below from *The Old Wives' Tale* is not directly modeled on Richardson—the chief influences upon it are French, and it could not, I think, have been written precisely as it is without Bennett's knowledge of Flaubert—but it belongs to the broad imaginative mode that Richardson initiated in which narration adheres to lived moments through consciousness. Gerald Scales, the singularly hollow young man who makes off with the romantically deluded Sophia Baines, has just entered Sophia's hotel room on the first night of their elopement:

Approaching her with factitious ease, he kissed her through her veil, which she then lifted with an impulsive movement, and he kissed her again, more ardently, perceiving that her ardour was exceeding his. This was the first time they had been alone together since her flight from Axe. And yet, with his wordly experience, he was naïve enough to be surprised that he could not put all the heat of passion into his embrace, and he wondered why he was not thrilled at the contact with her! However, the powerful clinging of her lips somewhat startled his senses, and also delighted him by its silent promise. He could smell the stuff of her veil, the sarsenet of her bodice, and, as it were wrapped in these odours as her body was wrapped in its clothes, the faint fleshly perfume of her body itself. Her face, viewed so close that he could see the almost imperceptible down on those fruit-like cheeks, was astonishingly beautiful; the dark eyes were exquisitely misted; and he could feel the secret loyalty of her soul ascending to him. She was very slightly taller than her lover; but somehow she hung from him, her body curved backwards, and her bosom pressed against his, so that instead of looking up at her gaze he looked down at it. He preferred that; perfectly proportioned though he was, his stature was a delicate point with him. (Book III, Chapter 1:1)

Some readers today may be put off by the touches of faded period style in the writing (most conspicuous in that "secret loyalty of her soul" which Scales feels "ascending to him"), but the passage as a whole is an admirable piece of literary craftsmanship. Bennett gives us a concise, pointed summary of Scales's conscious thoughts—the young man's pained awareness of himself as someone trying to play the part of the great lover, his anxiety about his own emotional and physical adequacy. At the same time we are offered discrete moments of Scales's immediate senuous apprehension of Sophia: his "startled" senses, in the ultimate proximity of an embrace, catch her misted eyes, the fine down on her cheeks, the scent of the fabrics she is wearing, the "faint fleshly perfume of her body itself." We have here another Lovelace implicating us in the sweet nearness of throbbing partners, though the rendering of detail is at once more minutely precise and less boldly disjunctive than in Richardson. A more essential departure from Richardson's technique is the presence of an inobtrusive but highly effective authorial commentator—

this, like the meticulous report of sensuous data, is Flaubertian—who passes implicit judgment on the character in the ostensibly straightforward summary of his consciousness. It is the evaluating commentator, for example, who tells us that Scales's ease is "factitious," and that he is sensitive about his shortness—a pathetic Napoleon, as it were, in the realm of Don Juans.

I suspect that the operation in the passage of this implicit authorial evaluation is the ultimate source of its distinctive strength, leading us beyond what it feels like to live through a certain experience to something of the "causal psychological insight" which C. P. Snow would like the novel to give us. Subtract the nice perception of Scales's moral character that informs the report of his consciousness and you are left with ardent lips, the sarsenet of bodices, and the sweet hot smell of woman's flesh—precisely the ingredients of the pulp-magazine fiction and genteel pornography that have assimilated and vulgarized the basic technique employed here by Bennett in which the narrative viewpoint is the character's consciousness. Though I would tend to be skeptical about the "exhaustion" of possibilities of expression in any literary mode, because genius so often manages to accomplish what is unlikely, it seems to me that the novelistic representation of consciousness is by now harder to do interestingly because it is so thoroughly familiar. Narration through the focus of a character's awareness has been done so often, by some of the most original writers but also by an immense number of irredeemably mediocre ones, that the most competent conventional employment of the technique may seem hackneyed, unimaginative. Arnold Bennett illustrates this point in retrospect: his rendering of Gerald Scales's experience, an obviously accomplished piece of writing in its own day and perhaps a little daring, too, may by now have acquired a certain staleness for many readers simply because its successors, good and mostly bad, have been legion.

The last passage I offer is from a contemporary novel

which evinces a decided interest in consciousness, but in a very different manner from that of the Richardsonian tradition, with very different aesthetic assumptions from those of the novelists who try to give the illusion of reality a perfect intactness in their fiction. Vladimir Nabokov's *Lolita* is a novel which, by the very nature of its subject, one might want to associate with Richardson rather than Fielding, but a careful reading of the book—or, for that matter, of almost any of Nabokov's novels—will, I think, reveal an interesting connection with Fielding's fiction of ostentatious artifice. Here is Humbert Humbert's first vision of the impossible adolescent whom he at once recognizes as the great passion of his life:

> It was the same child—the same frail, honey-hued shoulders, the same silky supple bare back, the same chestnut head of hair. A polka-dotted black kerchief tied around her chest hid from my aging ape eyes, but not from the gaze of young memory, the juvenile breasts I had fondled one immortal day. And, as if I were the fairy-tale nurse of some little princess (lost, kidnapped, discovered in gypsy rags through which her nakedness smiled at the king and his hounds), I recognized the tiny dark-brown mole on her side. With awe and delight (the king crying for joy, the trumpets blaring, the nurse drunk) I saw again her lovely indrawn abdomen where my southbound mouth had briefly paused; and those puerile hips on which I had kissed the crenulated imprint left by the band of her shorts—that last mad immortal day behind the "Roches Roses." The twenty-five years I had lived since then, tapered to a palpitating point, and vanished.[7]

The description of Lolita clings to the train of the protagonist's perceptions and recollections in a manner obviously different from anything in Fielding, but that free play with the possibilities of self-consciousness initiated in *Joseph Andrews* and *Tom Jones* is continued here, within the dizzying arena of Humbert Humbert's obsessed and splendidly poetic mind. In Nabokov as in Fielding the narrator makes us continually aware of his rhetoric, and Nabokov's rhetoric, like Fielding's, can often be construed as a mock-heroic instrument—that is, a language of the sublime applied with poised irony to objects which are far from sublime, at least according to traditional notions. Lolita is Humbert's own refulgent poetic creation, the Dulcinea of his noble and mad imagination, and what he gives us here is not so much a "report" of his consciousness upon first seeing her as the poem he has made out of that experience and out of her.

Humbert frequently calls attention to himself in the novel as writer and artificer ("A poet *à mes heures,* I composed a madrigal to the soot-black lashes of her pale-gray vacant eyes . . . Oh, that I were a lady writer who could have her pose naked in a naked light! . . . *This* Lolita, *my* Lolita, has individualized the writer's ancient lust" [8]); the formal elements of literary artifice stand out in the passage, as they do through the entire novel; and it is quite fitting that Humbert should elsewhere repeatedly apostrophize the Reader in the grand manner first cultivated by Fielding. Though the subject of this passage is erotic, it is, paradoxically, the language and not what it refers to that becomes the locus of sensual delight—Humbert gloats less over Lolita than over the ripe imagery and music she inspires, as in the succulent alliteration of "honey-hued shoulders" and "same silky supple bare back." As a result of the primary interest in the effects of language, there is a genuine chasteness in Nabokov's writing that becomes strikingly apparent when it is set against the depiction of inner states of arousal in the Richardsonian tradition. The coalescence of past and present summed up in the last sentence of the paragraph is neither Proustian nor Joycean but—the term is inevitable—Nabokovian: Humbert does not rehearse a psychological process but rather celebrates an act of art, admiring the beauty of his own visual metaphor in that concluding sentence, the lovely rhythm of its neatly mimetic decrescendo.

The place in this experience of the parenthesized fantasy on the kidnapped princess remains somewhat ambiguous. Is it a thought that actually flashed through Humbert's mind at the moment he first beheld Lolita's mole, the all-too-literary duplicate of Annabel's, his childhood love? Or is it rather an associative interpolation of Humbert, poet *à ses heures,* as he refashions his experience into poetry? The latter alternative seems more likely, but in any case, the parenthesis is another means of obtruding literary artifice into Humbert's vision of Lolita. The blaring horns and the joyfully weeping king of the fairy tale serve, as do the sundry analogous devices we have examined in Fielding, to evoke different possibilities of literary expression, to show forth teasing ambiguities in the relationship between literature and reality: like the Homeric fanfare in Molly Seagrim's churchyard battle, they heighten the action and also make it seem ridiculous, adding both a touch of fabled splendor and a note of self-mockery to Humbert's hunger for little girls. It should be apparent that this reflexive mode of fiction by its nature leads to self-irony in Nabokov's narrating protagonist as in Fielding's omniscient narrator. Typical of this self-irony is the fact that old Humbert, with his peculiar vice, casts himself here as a fairy-tale nurse opposite Lolita's role of innocent babe, that he beholds young beauty self-consciously through "aging ape eyes," that even a recollected act of erotic transport is described with a hint of facetiousness, the passionate Humbertian mouth "southbound" like some midnight express.

The self-irony of Nabokov's protagonist, like the irony through which Fielding imagines his personages, is, finally, an instrument for the fuller revelation of character. Though the term "morality," at least in its popular sense, would not appear to be especially apt for Nabokov's work, I think there is a moral as well as an aesthetic amplitude that results from his ironic method. Humbert's self-irony is a double irony through which he repeatedly makes us see him from divergent or opposing perspectives— a noble figure possessed by a grand passion, a pathetic little man nursing his sordid little vice; a tender, poetic soul victimized by a heartless, mindless, precociously vicious girl, or perhaps by what he calls his "Proustianized, Procrusteanized fancy"; and, in the great final revelations, an erotic egoist who has robbed Lolita of her childhood, reduced her to weeping herself secretly to sleep each night in an endless mobile prison of bleakly cozy motels.

Humbert in his Kumfy Kabin with Lolita is more than worlds away from Tom Jones in Mrs. Waters' bed at the Upton inn, but Nabokov shows a real kinship with Fielding in the fine balance of censure and sympathetic understanding achieved through his irony, in the fullness of humane outlook and the radiant exhibition of the power of conscious art which he makes manifest by his supremely serious playfulness. The awareness of the necessary condition of art as contrivance can have a liberating effect on a novelist, enabling him to view from a distance the swarming confusion of contemporary experience and fix it in the lucidity of a pattern. Though according to a common view of the novel a dogged commitment to the simulation of quotidian reality is indigenous to the genre, some distinguished novelists have not hesitated to move back and forth across the dividing line between art and reality—Fielding with his insinuation of acquaintances and associates into the fictional weave of his work; Joyce with his vast collage, that Homeric canvas pasted over with bits of real refuse from the Dublin streets and snippets of pages from the Dublin city directory; Nabokov the lepidopterist, who sends clue-bearing butterflies, literal and figurative, fluttering through the leaves of his novels.[9] This deliberate exposure of the splices that bind fiction and actuality is a manifesto of the writer's independence: rejecting the obligation to create a simple illusion of reality, he can toy with the real world in a more flexible kind of art, throwing reality into new perspectives by juxtaposing it in varying ways with the luminous contrivances of art.

To argue that Fielding has some bearing on the future of

the novel is not to suggest that he is in any way the wave of the future. Although one can find recent novels as different as *Henderson the Rain King, The Sot-Weed Factor,* and *An American Dream* that have adopted strategies of parody, allusion, and gravity-through-playfulness, they are hardly evidence that a new dominant mode of the novel is coming into being. The underlying assumption of this entire study has been that the novel was always more various than the critical definitions of it would lead us to believe, that there have been great traditions, not a Great Tradition, of the novel; and one would hope that this variety of orientations toward the fictional representation of contemporary life will be even more pronounced in time to come. At this particular point in literary history, Fielding is a writer emphatically worth rereading. Contemporary novelists, even when they can take over nothing from him directly, can at least learn from his achievement, so much finer than the stereotyped impression of it, that the possibilities of fiction are less restricted than we have sometimes assumed. If we often tend to think of the novel in terms of dramatic moral struggle, immersion in inner life, stubborn adherence to the factuality of quotidian experience—a complex of categories that derives ultimately from a Puritan world view—Fielding shows us a kind of novel which may be called artistocratic, in the broadest sense of the word, where fiction is graceful play, and graceful play becomes a means of moral and aesthetic revelation. It is not, at a time when existence seems to be such hard, grim work, the sort of novel that can comprehend all of what we think of as reality, but, in just such a trying historical moment, it may be more important than ever to write about the world in this way, too. The joyful self-consciousness of art offers, after all, a kind of play that is in one aspect redemptive—because it richly affirms the autonomy of the creative spirit of man.

NOTES
INDEX

NOTES

1. On the Critical Dismissal of Fielding

1. F. R. Leavis, *The Great Tradition* (Garden City, New York: Doubleday and Company, 1954), pp. 12–13.

2. F. T. Blanchard, *Fielding the Novelist* (New Haven: Yale University Press, 1926).

3. William Empson, "Tom Jones," *Kenyon Review*, 20 (Spring 1958); 217–249.

4. Ian Watt, *The Rise of the Novel* (Berkeley and Los Angeles: University of California Press, 1957), pp. 288–289.

5. "Je me retrouve en face de mes *Faux-Monnayeurs;* mais cette courte plongée dans Fielding m'éclaire sur les insuffisances de mon livre. Je doute si je ne devrais pas élargir le texte, intervenir . . . commenter." André Gide, *Le Journal des Faux-Monnayeurs* (Paris: Gallimard, 1927), p. 70.

6. *Johnsonian Miscellanies,* ed. G. B. Hill (Oxford: Clarendon Press, 1897), II, 189–190.

7. James Boswell, *Life of Johnson,* ed. G. B. Hill (Oxford: Oxford University Press, 1934), II, 48–49.

8. Frank Kermode, "Richardson and Fielding," *Cambridge Journal,* 4 (1950): 106–114.

9. Dorothy Van Ghent, *The English Novel: Form and Function* (New York: Rinehart and Company, 1953), pp. 45–63.

10. Samuel Johnson, *Works* (London: Oxford, 1825), V, 105–106.

11. Arnold Kettle, *An Introduction to the English Novel* (London: Hutchinson and Company, 1951), I, 76.

12. Wayne C. Booth, *The Rhetoric of Fiction* (Chicago: University of Chicago Press, 1961), p. 217.

13. Samuel Coleridge, *Works,* ed. W. G. T. Shedd (New York: Harper and Brothers, 1853), IV, 381.

14. The analogies between the structure of Fielding's novels and that of a legal case have been studied closely and suggestively by Hugh Amory in an as yet unpublished doctoral dissertation.

2. The Uses of Style

1. Martin C. Battestin has suggested to me that the words could also refer to the squatting position of London's beggars, whom Fielding, though a charitable man, regarded as a public nuisance. The excretory reference, however, seems to me more likely for Square at this moment.

2. I have analyzed at length the progress of one such passage in *Rogue's Progress: Studies in the Picaresque Novel* (Cambridge: Harvard University Press, 1964), pp. 82–103, and so I shall, like Fielding, "do violence to the luxuriance of [my] genius" and spare the reader further demonstration here.

3. *Irony in Tom Jones* (University, Alabama: University of Alabama Press, 1965), pp. 101–118. Miss Hutchens carefully documents the whole range of ironies attached to "prudence," but I am not entirely convinced of the usefulness of her distinction between "connotative" and "denotative" irony. The simple term "dialectic" seems to me a more accurate description of Fielding's ironies, and it is certainly more helpful in relating his ironic procedures to other aspects of his technique as a novelist.

4. Excellent things about Fielding's use of the persona have been written by Wayne C. Booth in *The Rhetoric of Fiction* (Chicago: University of Chicago Press, 1961), especially pp. 216–219, and so I shall comment only briefly here on the relevance of the persona to the style.

5. The "rude answer" is the conclusion to Rochester's poem, "To All Curious Criticks and Admirers of Metre." After a series of rhetorical questions, each beginning with "Have you seen," Rochester ends abruptly "If you have seen all this, then kiss mine [arse]." I am indebted to Martin Battestin for the reference.

6. Ian Watt, *The Rise of the Novel*, p. 254.

7. *The English Novel: Form and Function*, p. 80.

8. Shortly after writing this I discovered Martin C. Battestin's excellent essay on the analogies in artistic technique between the film and the novel, "Osborne's 'Tom Jones,': Adapting a Classic," *The Virginia Quarterly Review*, 42. 3 (Summer 1966): 378–393.

3. The Design of Character

1. *The Rise of the Novel*, p. 288.

2. "*Tom Jones,*" *Kenyon Review,* 20 (Spring 1958): 217–249.

3. Introduction to *Fielding: A Collection of Critical Essays,* ed. Ronald Paulson (Montclair, New Jersey: Prentice-Hall, 1962), p. 6.

4. Irvin Ehrenpreis, *Fielding: Tom Jones* (London: Edward Arnold Ltd., 1964), p. 40.

5. Fielding, *Complete Works,* ed. W. E. Henley (London: William Heineman, 1903), XIV, 283.

6. Martin C. Battestin, *The Moral Basis of Fielding's Art: A Study of "Joseph Andrews"* (Middletown, Conn.: Wesleyan University Press, 1959), especially, pp. 26f.

7. Martin Price has seen one aspect of this scheme in representing Tom as a kind of mean between Western and Allworthy, participating in the innocent carnality of one and the rational charity of the other. See *To the Palace of Wisdom* (New York: Doubleday and Company, 1964), p. 307.

8. Compare George Sherburn, "Fielding's Social Outlook," *Philological Quarterly,* 35 (1956): 8.

4. The Architectonic Novel

1. See W. B. Coley, "Gide and Fielding," *Comparative Literature,* 11 (1959): 13, and Maurice Johnson, *Fielding's Art of Fiction* (Philadelphia: University of Pennsylvania Press, 1961), pp. 113f.

2. The ironic correspondences between Strephon-Chloe and Joseph-Fanny have also been noticed by Dick Taylor, Jr., in "Joseph as Hero in *Joseph Andrews,*" *Tulane Studies in English,* 7 (1957): 92–97. His primary concern, however, is with how the scene brings Joseph out for the first time as an active male figure.

3. I. B. Cauthen, in "Fielding's Digressions in *Joseph Andrews,*" *College English,* 17 (1956): 379–382, takes another tack, attempting to justify the digressions as generalizing exempla of the comic vices of Vanity and Hypocrisy which Fielding names in his Preface.

4. Andrew Wright has made this observation in *Henry Fielding: Mask and Feast* (Berkeley and Los Angeles: University of California Press, 1965), p. 88.

5. Irvin Ehrenpreis, *Fielding: Tom Jones,* pp. 47f.

6. Mark Spilka, "Comic Resolution in Fielding's *Joseph Andrews,*" *College English,* 15 (1953): 11–19.

7. Andrew Wright, *Henry Fielding,* pp. 60–71, has made an attempt to describe the structural coherence of *Joseph Andrews,* but his account strikes me as mechanical in some ways and generally less than persuasive.

5. *Fielding's Problem Novel*

1. "Fielding and 'Conservation of Character,'" *Modern Philology*, 57 (1960): 245–259.

2. See George Sherburn, "Fielding's *Amelia:* An Interpretation," *ELH*, 3 (1936): 3–4; and compare L. H. Powers, "The Influence of the *Aeneid* on Fielding's *Amelia*," *Modern Language Notes*, 71 (1956): 330–336, and Maurice Johnson, *Fielding's Art of Fiction* (Philadelphia: University of Pennsylvania Press, 1961), pp. 139–156.

3. Coolidge, "Fielding and 'Conservation of Character,'" p. 250.

4. Morris Golden makes a related observation about the new treatment of character in *Amelia*, and about its sporadic application to both the Jameses, in *Fielding's Moral Psychology* (Amherst: University of Massachusetts Press, 1966), pp. 70–71.

5. The similarity of titles was suggested to me by Hugh Amory, who also points out that one take-off on *Shamela*, Fielding's parody of *Pamela*, was called *Shamelia*.

6. Samuel Richardson, *Correspondence*, ed. Anna Laetitia Barbauld (London: Richard Phillips, 1804), VI, 154.

6. *Fielding and The Future of The Novel*

1. José Ortega y Gasset, *The Dehumanization of Art and Notes on the Novel*, tr. Helene Weyl (Princeton: Princeton University Press, 1948), pp. 57–103.

2. Mary McCarthy, *The Humanist in the Bathtub* (New York: New American Library, 1964), pp. 190–191.

3. Norman Mailer, *Cannibals and Christians* (New York: Dial Press, 1966), pp. 238–239.

4. Kingsley Amis, *I Like It Here* (New York: Harcourt, Brace and Company, 1958), p. 185.

5. R. P. Blackmur, *A Primer of Ignorance* (New York: Harcourt, Brace and World, 1967), pp. 26–27.

6. "Science, Politics, and the Novelist," *Kenyon Review*, 23.1 (Winter 1961): 6.

7. *Lolita* (New York: Putnam, 1958), p. 41.

8. *Ibid.*, pp. 46–47.

9. This whole aspect of Nabokov has been finely described by Alfred Appel, Jr., in "Nabokov's Puppet Show," *The New Republic*, Jan. 14, 1967, pp. 27–30, and Jan. 21, 1967, pp. 25–32.

INDEX